DANCING AND CRYING

TO BE FREE

Order this book online at www.trafford.com
or email orders@trafford.com

Most Trafford titles are also available at major online book retailers.

Note for Librarians: A cataloguing record for this book is available from Library
and Archives Canada at www.collectionscanada.ca/amicus/index-e.html

Printed in Victoria, BC, Canada.

ISBN: 978-1-4269-1230-6 (Soft)
ISBN: 978-1-4269-1231-3 (Dust)
ISBN: 978-1-4269-1232-0 (e-book)

*We at Trafford believe that it is the responsibility of us all, as both individuals
and corporations, to make choices that are environmentally and socially sound.
You, in turn, are supporting this responsible conduct each time you purchase a
Trafford book, or make use of our publishing services. To find out how you are
helping, please visit www.trafford.com/responsiblepublishing.html*

*Our mission is to efficiently provide the world's finest, most comprehensive
book publishing service, enabling every author to experience success.
To find out how to publish your book, your way, and have it available
worldwide, visit us online at www.trafford.com*

Trafford rev. 07/16/2009

 www.trafford.com

North America & international
toll-free: 1 888 232 4444 (USA & Canada)
phone: 250 383 6864 ♦ fax: 250 383 6804 ♦ email: info@trafford.com

DANCING AND CRYING ©
* To Be Free *

BY: JOHN H. HALL

A BOOK OF ONE ACT

BLACK HISTORY PLAYS

INCLUDING:

FOREWORD ©

SLAVE SHIP ©
The Middle Passage

BURNT OFFERING ©
A Tower of Shadow

EULOGY: TO BE RISEN FROM PERDITION. ©

IN MEMORY OF:

Emanuel Pace
George Pace
Ida (Williams) Pace
Mary Elizabeth Pace
Johnnie Mae Gibson
Lora Anne Simpson (Tweety Bird)

Special thanks to God and his son Jesus.

For my children Johnnie & Lora & Grand children.

My siblings Charles, Linda, Leonard, Lora & Robert.

A special thanks to Pastor Robert & Iris Simpson & Family.
Including Grace Covenant Fellowship Ministries.
Round Rock, Texas

A special thanks to Pastor Norris Littles & Family.
Including Mountain of Faith Outreach Ministries.
Houston, Texas

A special thanks to Pastor Roosevelt and Mother B. Mitchell, including St. Mary's Holy Tabernacle.
Houston, Texas

FOREWORD

A few years ago I was a member of a circle of self styled Black History scholars. We debated many Black History myths and truths. Many times we debated issues while in heated disagreement, but as always, we debated in love, and also respect for all opinions. We debated issues that effected the Black Community, from the Slave Trade, up to this very day. We all agreed though that during this infamous Slave Trade, that over 'Two Hundred Million' African citizens had been captured, and most removed at gunpoint from their homes and from their sacred praying grounds. They were all transported by ships from the shores of Africa to the hemispheres of the world. Mostly the Western Hemisphere and more often than not, the United States of America.

Though many other countries participated in the trade of Africa's human treasures, that is a subject for future discussions. Knowing these circumstances is what impregnated me with the Plays that are before you now. The labor was long and painful. Because of such a dire need in our world community to know the true African American Experience, I travailed from some spiritual place within myself. Thus, these works as well as others were birthed out of my spirit. I've learned that when writing about atrocities such as this, very often one must, ones self, experience the same atrocities every time that ones hand and mind is put to pin and paper, regardless of the smells. Regardless of the inhuman treatment, causing suffering that is unparalleled, still the writer must write on.

I've been told that young people in 2009 /10 are not interested in Black History, or African American History. This history is, more descriptively, World and American History that involves the Continent of Africa and its citizens of conflict and contention with the world. That included the United States of America and it's Constitution, and even the constitutions and humanity of every country that has ever launched or landed even a single ship that has ever transported even a single human being for sale, or exploitation.

I believe that young people today can be a "catalyst" in the upsurge of a deeper understanding, and usher a more noble delivery of a much deeper truth, if they can identify with those in contention and conflict.

These works were written in part so that these who I claim that suffer herein , does not become even further victimized by a society that is moving towards indifference at speeds that are terrifying.

The agenda was sat by people like Sojourner Truth, Harriet Tubman Fredrick Douglas, Dred Scott, and many, many more named and unnamed, and many, many more recognized and unrecognized citizens of the world who was appalled at the thought of man adopting an immoral precedent that allowed the enslavement of another human being right before their eyes. This same agenda was sustained by Dr. Martin Luther King Jr. , and was realized to a larger extent by our election of President Barack Obama. But there is unfinished work that lie in the middle ground that must be filled in by those of us who are every day citizens who populate the cities, towns, universities, societies, fraternities, sororities, corporations, churches, of all denominations, ministries, internet bloggers, and even every concerned Individual. If you want to feel the earth move at your command as it moved at your command in electing President Barack Obama, this is a noble cause. Candidate Obama called upon us and we all responded. Now we must call upon him as president to respond to this historical travesty that continue to go un repaired.

It is my responsibility to deliver to you an uncompromising ideal. An ideal that fall at the feet of every civilized human. Holding each human being as their other brothers keeper. I have for many years been appalled at the things that has been accepted in 2009/10 and beyond as passe'. I awoke from a vision advised that the whole truth has not yet been told. Since I feel so strongly appalled about this lack of whole truth, I have taken the responsibility of speaking to the issue of the African American experience that continue to lie in conflict and contention.

Far too often the Issue of Slavery has been painted with one broad brush stroke. I contend that this was not only the rape of a continent, but was also the violent assault and the murder of peaceful individuals who had names and who are ancestors of some who live among us today. We can't just leave them behind as though they did not exist or had somehow brought this on themselves.

There are only brief entries in the Slave Ship Captain's logs, and subsequent census reports that list the living, breathing human beings simply as part of the ships cargo or stock property "owned" by another man. My point is that, getting to "that place" in the minds and beings of the Slave Owners and Slave Proponents, must have been a greater and more hazardous distance to travel than navigating the dangerous waters of the entire middle passage itself.

By the sheer volume of Slave Ships and countries involved in this Slave Trade Atrocity, it is not at all possible for one to have heard about every drama that unfolded during this period of decay in our moral national character. Enter the author of these works and the many tattle tale *characters that continue to stand up and tell me and other tattle tale Writers their painful and sensational accounts of what really went down during this short but ever electrifying moment in our Black History.*

I submit to you that these African citizens had no script to survive by nor to die by, nor did they have the benefit of hindsight. To each individual, their plight was unprecedented. Many Slaves died from illnesses that they didn't understand. They knew though that if they were unfortunate enough to get sick, that the Dr. wasn't Coming. Though many died from loneliness, we dare not fail to mention the thousands upon thousands who sacrificed themselves because they just refused to live under the conditions of Slavery.

For those who argue that we enslaved each other, of course there were wars among the many, many tribes of the many countries of Africa. Even wars of very close rival kingdoms, as in all early societies. What I am appalled by is that they (the African citizens) had to encounter such blind injustice and such brutal disrespect to such a long established culture of royalty, verified by generation, too many to count. Inferior??

I submit to you that if the middle passage could speak!
If the spirits of witnesses could speak!
If the rich southern soil that has absorbed the blood, sweat and tears of a degraded people could speak!
If the beautiful plantations of the south could speak!
If the four walls of the Slave huts could speak!
If the four walls of the shameful bed huts could speak!
If the returning wind, the rain and the sun could speak!
If the reluctant tree branches that bore the weight of a despised people by their necks could speak!

If the rivers of waters that run and hide in the seas could speak!

If the worn shackles of our souls and spirits could speak!

If the cotton that has returned to the earth could speak!

If the spirit of a reluctant currency, spent to purchase the souls of a people could speak! It would tell stories of how one deflated treasure was exchanged for a more valuable, human treasure that "still" ….

If the chronicles of stark injustices could speak, they would proudly whisper stories of a people who has an indomitable spirit to resist when there was no hope evident.

If the spirits of the enlightened sons of Southern Gods could speak!

*They would all compare stories of a people who for generations upon generations has **danced, loved, and cried to be free!***

I believe that there is something innately real about a human spirit that is held in bondage! There was always a subtle resistance among Slaves that only those involved could understand or even detect! The root of which may live even to this very day. There was always a silent language of resistance that lived in even the most docile of House Slaves. Surly we have to believe that it would be impossible to move two hundred million people around in the world without Gods knowledge, as this is movement on a biblical scale. I dare not question God, but I do question my fellow man. The fellow man that I overheard trying to convince others that the issue of Slavery was not really as bad as Slavery opponents try to make it seem, while trying to make the nightmare of reparations disappear from all of our vocabularies and our minds. The fellow man was concerned about what reparations would do to our fragile economy.

Nothing, I said, except raise the economy to where it would have been if the money that is owed to our ancestors had been paid to them when they had finished the work.

But those who did this to you are no longer alive, 'he said. "Their spirit lives' was my answer to that! So, what does all this mean? Why in 2009/10 do I find it necessary to open up old Slavery wounds, 'I am sometimes asked'. They are wounds but they are not old. There is suppuration and we have to Learn quickly how to treat our own wounds because no one else knows how.

There is a danger looming over the African American and world community like a dangerous toxic fog. The danger is of this African American Community, even the world community, in all of it's passion, but also in all of it's sometimes serial detachments, loosing it's passion for the real history of our selves. We should by no means let sleeping dogs lie. The Bible tells us that 'Our People are "destroyed for lack of knowledge". There is a knowledge of our entire selves that must never die! So we absolutely must stop bringing physical and mental harm, including death, and destruction to ourselves. We must define ourselves and our own needs.

This will free us completely of the fear of physical abuse and even the fear of death at the hands of ourselves, elevating us higher than ever before in the eyesight of our God, thus raising us to a higher level among mankind.

*I sincerely hope that you enjoy reading these works and begin to, and or continue to see your brothers and sisters and yourselves as who you really are .***Just another human being who is Dancing and Crying to be Free.**

Rev. John H. Hall

SLAVE SHIP [©]
The Middle Passage

THE PLAY

BY:

JOHN H. HALL

CAST OF CHARACTERS

IDA HASEU

WASHI JOMO (BONE MAN)

EKIDA

KUBA

IBONI WOMAN

LITTLE GIRL

CAPTAIN & SHIP'S CREW

TIME Year Of Our Lord during early Slave Trade

PLACE The Middle Passage

SETTING Slave Ship

The action of this play takes place on an old, wooden, crudely constructed Slave Ship. This Slave Ship is rising and falling with the giant waves of the Un harnessed Atlantic Ocean. Throughout this action, there are the sounds of waves striking the sides of this wooden vessel. Throughout, there are faint sound of African drum rhythms and the traditional sounds of African life.

This Slave Ship is in route to the Western Hemisphere. The Slave Ship's human cargo is 358 African citizens that has been violently captured and forced away from the shores of Africa. This Slave Ship is powered by historical winds from the North, East, South, and West, blowing away lives, hopes, and dreams, deferring them fully, en masse. There are young men and old men. young women and old women. There are babies and pre- adolescent children to young adult hood. Some of the Slave Captives are chained around the sides of the ship racks. Some of the Slave Captives are chained to the floor level by their necks, some by their ankles, and some are not chained at all. These that are not chained are huddled together, using only themselves as shelter in the leaking bottom of the old Slave Ship. Some of the Slave Captives are clothed and some are not. These who are clothed are so clothed only covering their private parts.

The setting is the inside of this old wooden Slave Ship and the top deck. There are several broken and rotten rafters hanging low in places that define the ceiling of the under deck . There are stairs that lead down into the under deck from the top deck. There are several prominent patches on the inner sides of the Slave Ship, that continue to leak violently throughout the entire play. The unchained Slave Captives separate themselves according to their tribes. They sit and lie here in the prevailing wet stench of urine, and excrement, that makes the already thick air even thicker.

I know that this is true because I am there! The Slave Captives hail from the West Coast of Africa, Central Africa, Northwest Africa, South west Africa, and many, many other areas and from many, many, great tribes and countless, nameless villages throughout the Continent of Africa.s.

At times the African drum rhythms and the traditional African sounds are louder than other times, depending on the intensity of the action of the play. There is also a constant sound of chanting and traditional rituals sung in the many, many native tongues and dialects of the many, many great tribes of Africa. Some of the Slave Captives are great men and great women of high position in their tribes and in their regions. Some of these Slave Captives are kings, some are queens and rulers in their beloved Africa. Some of the African Slave Captives are just ordinary citizens that love their country and love their way of life. They hail from such tribes as the Fellatah, the Bantu, the Mali, the Watusi, the Zulu, the Dingo, the Fulani, the Iboni, and many, many other tribes, nobility.

Act: 1

Scene 1

There are loud voices and loud scraping sounds coming from towards the top deck. The hatch slides slowly open half it's length. A hand and an arm can be seen. The hand and arm is not like the hands and arms that the Slave Captives are accustomed to seeing. As the hatch opens wider, several white skinned men can be seen. One white skinned man can be heard screaming obscenities at the other white skinned men. The screamer stands with a long sword in his hand and waves it around in a threatening manner. He is standing next to an older white skinned man who has his arms folded behind his back. These two men are wearing long black coats, that almost touch the floor of the deck. The spirit of cruelty is emitting from their voices and their demeanor. The entire unchained Slave Captive population moves away from the hand and voices that has been so violating and cruel to them. The hand lowers two ropes that has attached to them a large container of many large fish, and an equally large container of drinking water. The pots hits the floor of the Slave Ship under deck with a muffled thud. For the brief time that the hatch is opened, the life sustaining fresh air burst into the damp, stuffy foul smelling compartments that make up the under deck.

For this brief time, the constant stench of blood, urine sweat, and excrement seems to reverse. The fresh air add new dimensions to their weakened black bodies. The Slave Captives scurry away from the half cooked fish and water containers as they come to rest at the bottom of the steps that lead up to the top deck. The black bodies desperately seek to avoid any contact with the fish, the water, and the hand that lowered them into the hatch. The sounds, rhythms and chants intensify, sweeping the entire Slave Captive population again and again. The sounds of the Slave Captives chains and chants can be heard from as far away as the reluctantly departed shores of Africa.

Now the hatch slides slowly shut with a loud, screeching sound, that cut off the fresh air supply. For a single moment in time and space, all noise stops. Even the sound of the waves that strike the underside of this bobbing Slave Ship.

A silhouetted figure moves in the rear of the Slave Ship. Coming out from among the tribes of Slave Captives a man appear. He is unchained. This silhouetted figure moves with authority, and with a blitzing effect. It is a figure of a man, moving around the sitting and the crowding men that are groping around in the food and water.

His graying hair seems to illuminate the blackness of his face. His sudden movement brings with him over 700 eyes that are fixed on him and are absolutely certain that there is something extraordinary about this man. He pushes and finally makes his way to the front of the Slave Ship where the half cooked fish and water has been lowered into the under deck. He is a lean man and is well built. There are recent scars on his cheek and arms that speak of his resistance to being captured. This man is King and Chief of the great Nigeritian race of people, of which all of these great tribes both great and small, are a part.

Boasting the largest tribal populations within the borders of most of the countries that lie within the continent of Africa. This great man is called King Chief Ida Haseu, educated at feet of his father the great Quam Haseu, and the many great leaders of beloved Africa's past and present. Chief Haseu has managed to remain anonymous to all even to the Slave Captors, since being in captivity for fear of sure death at the hands of this evil man. Ida Haseu, seeing that some tribes are beginning to aggressively move ahead of others in less aggressive tribes for the fish and water. He stops them.

Ida Haseu

All of you, stop! Stop your greed!

Ida Haseu takes charge, pointing to a woman in the crowd of unchained Slave Captives, who seem to be disinterested in all that is taking place. Pointing and looking intendedly at the woman.

You! Woman! What is your name and what tribe are you from.

Getting to her feet, Ekida replies in a low voice.

Ekida

I am Ekida. I myself am of the fallatah people. But my husband Elba was the chief of the Iboni people!

Looking sadly.

He died at the hands of this evil man!

Reminiscences.

We were so happy! We had such a beautiful life! All the Iboni people call me their wife. They say that I am married to 'all ' of the Iboni people.

Smiling, getting emotional.

Oh, I'm sorry. I usually a much stronger woman, but you must Understand, I have lost so much.

Ida Haseu

After a brief silence.

I do understand Ekida. Truly you are an adventurous woman. A Fallatah woman living with the Iboni people.

smiling

And yes, this evil man has been brutal to us all. You are brave Ekida, but there are many brave that are among us, that share in our tragedy.

Looking around at the many people who are chained at the various levels and who are unchained and are sitting in the blood, urine, tears, vomit and excrement.

We must continue to survive at all costs. Ekida, I am Ida Haseu, King Chief of the Nigeritian Race, of which you and your deceased husband are a part. I have known your deceased husband Elba very well.

Looking pleasantly surprised.

Ekida

Oh, I have heard much of you also. I am so glad that you have known my husband Elba.

Smiling! Reminiscences!

Ida Haseu

Aaa yes! I know the Iboni people very well. Your husband Elba and I have sat on many councils together. Now, today, we are faced with another life or death question.

Looking again at the sorrow around them.

We must survive this journey!

Ekida

Flushed with pride as she looks upon the royalty of king Chief Ida Haseu.

Yes, King Haseu I agree. It's most important that we all survive this journey.

Ida Haseu

Looking down at the big pots of half cooked fish and water.

Ekida, take this fish and divide it equally among all that are here. Take another woman with you and also pour a drink into each of their cupped hands. You must first feed those who are chained in place. Also ask those who are unchained to visit those who are chained in place, and ask them who can, to speak their own dialect languages to them.

Ida Haseu then moves away like a giant cat and blends in again into the huddled mass of black bodies. The stench is almost unbearable. Ekida, along with other women proceed to follow the honorable instructions of honorable King Chief Ida Haseu. The women divide the fish equally among the Slave Captives, beginning first with those who are chained in place. Ekida makes sure that everyone on the Slave Ship has a small portion to eat, and drink .as It is not known when the hand of so much contention will again drop more fish and water into this toxic under deck.

The sounds of religious harmony and chains clinging and chants from the Iboni tribe is gaining so much rhythm that the other tribes begin to join in and begin to cling their chains and chant each their own religious harmonies.

After countless days on the ocean has passed, Ekida moves through the huddled masses of Slave Captives. Ekida is very sad. She finds Ida Haseu and speaks to him.

Ekida

King Haseu, the Iboni people has refused to eat the fish, and they will not drink the water. This is the second time that they have refused to eat and drink and their bodies are growing weaker. The first time that they refused to eat, I divided their fish among the Iboni children, though the older Iboni children has refused to eat also.

Ida Haseu looks up sharply, but does not speak.

I have told the Iboni people who you are and that you will know the right thing to do.

The Slave Ship takes a big roll, fighting back at the giant waves that seem to threaten the very integrity of the ship's structure. All of the Slave Captives lean with the movement of the Slave Ship in it's fight to stay in one piece.

Voices of the Captain and ship's crew can be heard again, shouting above them on the upper deck.

Voices

Hold it! Hold it! Hold on to it! My God man! You there! Yes you! Stop what you are doing! Stand away man!

If you ever do that on my ship again I will feed you to the sharks! Or better still, I'll feed you to the darkies!

Ok! Ok! We're going to start all over again from the beginning. Stand by! Stand by! Can any one say "The captain is on deck"?

Command is repeated by the crew.

"The captain is on deck"
All commands from the captain are to be... what??

All

"Repeated"!
Ok then,, Run up the storm mast!

Crew repeats the command.

"Run up the storm mast"
You there man! Put your hand to your work! And you there, grab that tackle gear and move it out of your way!

Get ready! Get ready! Listen to my commands. Stand by,,, Stand by,,,
Loose the rudder bands!!

The crew repeats the captain's commands.

"Loose the rudder bands!!"
Now hoist the main sail to the wind!

The crew repeats the captain's commands.

"Hoist up the main sail!"
You there! Why are you just standing there, put your hand to that rope, or I will flog you for your supper.

The thoughts of the Slave captives return to their own dilemma.

Ida Haseu

Did you explain to them the importance of their survival?

Ekida

Yes, I have said all these things to the Iboni people.

Ida Haseu

Now standing, facing the mass of black bodies. Getting their attention.

Listen to me countrymen, please! Listen to me! There is no doubt that more of us will die here, and we will sadly have to carry their bodies to the top side, as before. We all morn for them now. And also we must believe that the ten men that were summoned to the upper deck, will not return to us. We must morn for them also.

There is no doubt that more of us will die of sickness because of these conditions that we are subject to. We could even die from sadness, I too miss our land and our homes and our families even our way of life. But as your leader I must say to you that those of you who have a will to continue in this life, must nourish your bodies to survive. We must not die from starvation when there is food to eat!

Ida Haseu walk among the seated Slave Captives.

All that we have to eat right now is the fish that is dropped to us! We- must- not- hate- the- fish! Please understand my words! If we are to come back to our land when we have organized ourselves and are numbered again, we must first begin our fight by surviving here today. We can and we must rebuild our lives! We can rebuild our empires!

For this, my countrymen, we need for each and every one of us to survive. Please you must hear me! We must live!

As a result of the direct plea from Ida Haseu, the Iboni people did eat.

After many more days on the ocean has passed and many more days of pain and uncertainty, Ekida again comes to Ida Haseu in sadness.

Ekida

King Haseu, during our religious ceremonies, the Iboni people have determined that it is not the will of God that they shall live in captivity like an animal.

Ida Haseu

Angrily striking the side of the Slave Ship with his hands, speaking to Ekida.

Don't they know that it's hard enough to live through this middle passage? Go back to them you must persuade them that there must be a will to survive, or we will all die in our spirits.

Ekida

With a gesture of refusal.

I have tried to reason with the Iboni. They wait to see if I will walk with them. I understand them, and they believe that I am one of them, though I am only married to them.

King Haseu, the Iboni are a proud people. They are a strong, brave people, but they refuse to live in captivity. The minds of the Iboni People are made up.

Kuba

Young Iboni warrior walking up to Ida Haseu and Ekida.

King Ida Haseu, our sister is right. This is the way that all Iboni feel, including me.

In the circle of wise men I have heard it said many times that no one will ever be able to make a slave out of an Iboni man, woman, nor even an Iboni child.

I have heard 'you' say these words also Chief Ida Haseu. Before we are reduced to the dishonor of slavery and work our lives away in another land, for another people, we would rather die. Right here, and right now, Chief Haseu we are ready to die, all of us.

Ida Haseu

Looking supprised at the young warrior.

You seem to know quite a lot for one so young in age! Just who are you son? What is your name?

Ekida

Apologetically

Please forgive me! I am so sorry. I have forgotten my manners.

Introducing Ida Haseu to tribesman - Warrior, Kuba.

Chief Haseu, this is Anwon Kuba. He is a young tribal official in my deceased husbands army of tribesmen. Kuba is young but he is very dedicated. He is sworn by tribal law for every tribal members continuous safety and integrity.

Ida Haseu

Unimpressed

Yes, I know of this law very well, since It was 'I' who wrote these tribal laws myself.

Ekida

I have told tribesman Kuba all about you, Chief Haseu.

Ida Haseu

Greetings Tribesman Anwon Kuba, I know your family very well, but I must say that I do not know you. Maybe it is because you were out -side playing when I spoke with your fathers. You are too young to know so much, or even to repeat what you may have heard.

Kuba

Standing arrogantly.

I know that I would rather jump into the ocean and 'die' at the mouth of the great fish, and let the great tides wash my body and my spirit back to the only land that I love. Back to the shores of Africa! This is what all the Iboni people feel! What about you King Haseu?

Ida Haseu

Continues to mock Tribesman Anwon Kuba.

Tell me young Kuba, what else do you know that the rest of us should know?

Kuba

Standing defiantly in the presence of King Haseu.

We have learned from the old Iboni man who throws the bones, that the things that lie in wait for us at the end of this voyage is much more painful than the things that we now experience.

Ida Haseu

Ida Haseu can feel his heart rate increasing.

Who is this old man that you speak of? Speak quickly man! Who is this one who you say throws the bones?

Kuba

encouraged that he has gotten King Haseu's undivided attention.

He is Washi Jomo, the wise man of the Iboni people. He knows that many more of us will die on this journey!

He knows that more of us will be thrown into these waters for this evil mans own sport.

The Bone man also says that there is a place at the end of this voyage that is called Ameka that is a new world. And this will be a world of hatred for us. A place of deceit and cruelty for us, but not for other men who...

Ida Haseu

Interrupting Kuba.

Aaaa, so you think that this old man who throws the bones is right, do you?

Kuba

Yes, I believe him, and so does one hundred other Iboni men, women and children.

Ida Haseu

Then take me to this Washi Jomo, this Bone Man!

Ida Haseu, Ekida, and Kuba begin to make their way through the crowds of unchained Slave Captives, on their way to see this Washi Jomo, this Bone Man. Ida Haseu can feel the eyes of the entire Slave Captive population following their every move, until every one is startled at the loud screams of Ekida.

Ekida

EEEEEEEEK! EEEEEEEEK! Stop the woman! Stop her please. Someone Please stop her!

Ekida sees an Iboni woman that is attempting to end her young child's life by bashing the child against the side of the Slave Ship wall. Ekida is total horror. Ekida grabs the child's body, holding it close to her own body.

The Iboni woman is still holding on to the child's feet, struggling to retain control of the child. Ida Haseu is trying to wrestle the child away from the Iboni

Woman. The child is covered with urine, excrement and vomit, and is crying it's eyes out, but not really understanding just how close to death that it actually is.

Ida Haseu

Stop! Stop! Woman, let go of this child right now! I command you. Hold on to the child Ekida! Don't let it drop to the floor.

Iboni Women

Crying and pulling away from those who are preventing her from the act of murder against her child. Striking at King Haseu, and Ekida.

I would rather see my child dead, and I myself, than to live in a strange land as a Slave Woman. The Bone Man has told us the truth! There is no reason for any of us to live and suffer through all of this, and still be enslaved to someone.

Ida Haseu

Iboni Woman! Listen to me! If we must die, so be it! But we can never die at our own hand. God would not be pleased with any of us for letting this act of murder against our children. go on forth.

Iboni Woman

Crying while speaking.

Where is God now, King Haseu? Where is our God now while we rot in our own urine and our own waste? Please leave me alone! I mean it when I say that I would rather see my child dead and I myself, than to see us live in this way. We are Iboni people King Haseu, we are Iboni!

My son here,,,

Pointing at her other child sitting in the urine, vomit and excrement.

Continueing.

My son was born to be a warrior, not a Slave!

Ida Haseu

Looking around at the unchained Slave Captives who form a tight circle around them. Ekida and Kuba both also appear to be overcome with horror.

Speaking to the people who surround them.

Why do no one try to stop this woman from committing murder to her own child?

Ida Haseu let go of the child into Ekida's arms. Ekida gives the child to a woman standing in the crowd of black bodies. Ekida, Ida Haseu and Kuba can see the disinterest on the faces of the entire Iboni tribe.

Ida Haseu realize that it is true that all the Iboni tribe would rather be dead than to be enslaved by this evil man who drive this evil Slave Ship.

Ida Haseu's expression shows that even though he disagree with their method,,, he does somehow understand the spirit inside them pulling them away from conforming to their call to Slavery.

In his mind Ida Haseu tries fight the force pulling him to rationalize.

The sorrow of the Iboni tribe seems to know no bounds. The Iboni and all other tribes begin to sit again an rows and rows and begin rocking back and forth again chanting and singing old traditional songs. The faint sounds of African drum rhythms and the traditional sounds of African life continue, as well as the sounds of the giant waves that continue to strike the side of the Slave Ship. They continue in route to the Western Hemisphere with a human cargo of about 350 African Citizens, powered by historical winds from the North, East, South and West. blowing away lives, dreams, and hopes. Deferring them, en masse

Vibrations from every soul seems to cry out from one side of the Slave Ship to the other. From the top rafters down to the urine and the excrement that they all walk and sit in. . We are lost! We are lost! We are lost forever, they seem to think in one thought.

The entire Slave ship of sweating black bodies are shelters for each other, sweating violently against each other while sitting on the wet mildewed floor of the badly leaking Slave Ship, sitting in the blood, sweat ,urine, vomit and excrement mixed with the waters of the ocean.

Ida Haseu

We must survive! Survival is our only hope to ...

END OF SCENE ONE

Act: 1

Scene: 2

Scene two opens on the same Slave Ship under deck as in scene one. the same hardships that existed in scene one continue to exist in scene two. Surly the seasons has changed. There is a new coldness now, and a new dampness caused by the leaking patches on the sides of the Slave Ship and the urine , the vomit and the excrement that mingles with the ocean waters that leak into the Slave Ship's under deck. The horrible smells and presence of the urine and the excrement continue to dominate the air and the overall environment as they mingle and splash with the roll and movement of the Slave Ship. I know that this is true because I am here.

Also the sounds of rhythmic drums and the traditional sounds of Africa continue through out this scene. This new coldness of the waters, the cold air, and the smells of the urine and the excrement rush through the under deck touching, then moving all of their senses to an even newer and higher spiritual level. These of this Slave Captive population who are unchained, move even closer to each other in order to better resist this new enemy, cold and the fear of a new unknown.

The action begin as Ida Haseu, Ekida, and Kuba are making their way to the rear of the Slave Ship in order to speak to this Iboni Bone Thrower. The pocket of Slave Captives forms a tight wedge of black bodies around Ida Haseu, Ekida, and Kuba, following them as they move through to the back corner of the Slave Ship.

Ida Haseu

*Finally arriving at the bone throwers station in the rear
of the Slave Ship, looking sternly at Washi Jomo as he
is being pointed out to King Haseu.*

So! You are he who throws the bones! You are he who
has turned this vessel upside down on these waters!
Tell me the things that you have told these honorable
Iboni people that has confused them to the point of their
deaths.

Washi Jomo

King ,Chief, Ida Quam Haseu, a fathers son. 'It' is
you! It is so good to see you.

You have always lead our people well.

Ida Haseu

Taking a long, good look at Washi Jomo.

Yes, right into the bowels of this Slave Ship.

Washi Jomo

No one blames you for our fate Chief Haseu.

Ida Haseu

Maybe not, but I myself take the full responsibility
for our fate.

Washi Jomo

I had heard that you were on this Slave Ship, but I
dare not leave my hiding place, because it is much too
painful to look into the faces of those who ask me so
many agonizing, painfully uncompromising questions.
And also, surely this evil man will kill me if he knew for
one moment that I was on this vessel, 'unchained'.

There is a moment of laughter among the two men.

Ha-ha-ha-ha-ha-ha-ha-ha-ha.

Ida Haseu

What you say is true. I too have managed to remain anonymous myself, except for a few incidents that were unavoidable.

Washi Jomo

Reminiscing.

Young Haseu! I had been in councils with your father many, many times, before his departure. Too many times to count actually. A very fine and brave man your father was. I see that you are just as he. Believe me when I say that your father lives through you, in your dedication to the people of Africa.

Ida Haseu

Thank you for your compliments about my father, This is good talk for us but this young warrior,

Turning to Kuba.

has told me of things that your bones has said to the Iboni and to the other tribes. Can your bones speak of these things again? This time to me?

Washi Jomo

Perhaps the bones will speak again. The bones are our friends. They informs us in times of prosperity, also in times of trouble. The bones are of the animals that we respect, love and fear. As you might imagine O' King they all have their own points of view and fears.

Ida Haseu

Then throw the bones and let them tell us what has happened to the ten men who were taken to the top deck. The ten that has not returned to us, that causes us to continue to morn. Let the bones first tell us that! And we will all listen to their words.

Looking startled, then into the wide eyes of King Haseu, feeling his seriousness, feeling his pain. but does not speak immediately. Ida Haseu continuing impatiently.

For God's sake man, throw the bones!

Washi Jomo looking around at the anticipating black faces that are growing more and more anxious concerning the out come information of the ten men who were summoned to the top deck.

Washi Jomo

Is this a trial for me O' King? Is this a trial for these sacred bones? Or do you just mock me?

Ida Haseu

In defense of his inquiry.

Of course I do not mock you Bone Man! Let your bones speak to all of us, for our own sake.

Washi Jomo

Speaking slowly and with a trembling voice.

My feet ache! My head is in constant pain! I have never in my old life smelled such a smell as we are forced to endure day and night on this Slave Ship.

The sounds of splashing now mix with the sounds of the African drums and the traditional sounds of Africa perfectly as Washi Jomo, Ida Haseu, Kuba and Ekida slosh through the blood, urine, tears, vomit and excrement following Washi Jomo, making their way to the hiding place of the old sacred bones.

It is not good that our feet and our bodies stay wet day and night, you know. We are not a water people, are we?

Looking around at the group that follows him, and the pocket of black bodies and faces that surround them.

Do you know that The Bantu people and the Zulu people take turns holding their children up out of the waters to keep them dry. Do you know that, O' King?

Ida Haseu continue to look Washi Jomo directly into his eyes.

But the Iboni people has chosen to do nothing to survive. The Iboni want there to be an end to all of this madness. They wish to die on this Slave Ship! Now!

The group arrive at the hiding place of the sacred bones. The Bone Man takes the sacred bones out of their hiding place and begin to hum an old traditional African song used in the ritual of Bone Throwing. The Sacred bones are wrapped tightly in an old tattered cloth. This Bone Man moves slowly and deliberately, removing the bones. He carefully spread the tattered cloth in one of the few dry places that remain on the floor level of this Slave Ship. The Bone Man takes all of the bones fully into his thick, worn hand palms the way that he has a thousand times in his old, rich life. Washi Jomo remembers his challenge. Never before has Washi Jomo been so blatantly challenged as to the accuracy of his report from the bones secret chamber of wisdom, as he is being challenged by this King Ida Haseu.

Ida Haseu turn away for a long second as Washi Jomo shake the bones briskly in his palms, listening for the familier sounds of their authority to proceed with their report. Ida Haseu turns to face the bones at the very second that the Bone Man releases the bones briskly and with great skill to the old tattered cloth. Ida Haseu is no stark stranger to this art of Bone Throwing, but he has never employed a Bone Thrower in his many administrations. His mind entertains the thought of maybe he should have. Ida Haseu turn his full attention to the bones upon hearing the bones strike each other again and again and finally coming to their resting place on the old tattered cloth. Ida Haseu reach out to touch the bones as they come to their complete stop. Washi Jomo blocks the hand of Ida Haseu, then push his hand away.

Washi Jomo

No King! You must never interfere with the bones. The bones know who you are, but they will not bargain with you just because you are King. These bones will speak only the truth to you!

Ida Haseu

Tell us then what the bones say to us, Bone Man.

Ida Haseu beginning to feel faint as he look deeply at the bones then at the eyes of Washi Jomo, the Bone Thrower. He is now holding onto the shoulder of young Kuba.

Washi Jomo

Speaking slowly and deliberately.

There is a man on the topside - an older man.

Looking directly into the eyes of Ida Haseu.

The bones say that this man is the King of Evil. The brutality of this man has only increased his appetite for more and more brutality, changing him into a man as of an animal. The bones know this man all too well. This old man folds himself with his arms folded up behind his back like this.

Trying to fold his arms as such, but is unable to.

This is a double mined man with double thoughts and double acts.

Ida Haseu

Impatiently

Tell us about the young men who were summoned to the topside, Bone Man.

Washi Jomo

Please, be patient and quiet O' King! I must hear also as the bones speak.

After considering the bones for another long moment.

When the young men are called to the topside, this old man that I speak of, removes his sword from it's sheath. He then causes the young men to walk to the edge of the ship. Those who hesitate to fall into the waters, some he pierce in their sides causing them to fall into the waters

The Bone Man looks harder at the bone patterns as they lay un effected by the strong stench of the urine and the excrement.. A child is heard vomiting up his recently eaten fish again. The Bone Man is careful to not make a mistake in his report of the words that the bones speak.

All that are pierced in their side fall into the waters and are overcome by the waters and the great waves of this ocean. The fish, great and small do follow this Slave Ship and they wait for the next man to fall into the waters as their food. This man then catch the fish that follow this Slave Ship.

Washi Jomo looks perplexed at times as though he is hearing some of these revelations for the first time himself.

This is the fish that this man feed to us now. Our young men are the bait for the fish! We are their bait! This man plan to have only a numbered amount of Slaves left when we reach the shores of this new land. We are the bait, but the woman is more a value to them for sale.

Ida Haseu is utterly stunned. He can feel an increasing weakness in his stomach. He feel the need to sit, but he

forces himself to remain standing though holding on to the shoulder of Kuba. Ekida is crying louder as are the other women who are riding on this Slave Ship.The Black bodies that form the tight pocket around Ida Haseu, Washi Jomo, Kuba, and Ekida see what is happening in the rear of this Slave Ship from a hypnotic state of being. Those who are chained in place listen, straining to hear every word, forming images in each of their own minds, resolving them, allowing prisoners of every un translated word and phrase their discretion that dance and cry in their freedom. Freedom, compensating for every sound and every word coming from a space that they cannot see, but do no less experience.

Ida Haseu no longer feel the need to question any of this startling and assailing information. All things said by this Bone Man add to truth. The Bone Man stops for a moment, wipes his eyes and face. There is a new tired feeling now covering Ida Haseu, Washi Jomo and all of those who surround them. Ida Haseu manage to smile a half smile at Ekida, Kuba and Washi Jomo. They all smile slightly then quickly cut their smiles off.

Ida Haseu

I must go now! I must go! I will come again when I have rested and have digested the fruit of this evil man.

Washi Jomo

I understand O' King. Please come again when you have rested. You shall find me here, waiting.

Ida Haseu turns to walk away as Washi Jomo slowly rolls up the bones in their cloth, putting them away. Speaking to Ida Haseu.

King Haseu!

King Haseu stops.

Stick out your tongue! Yes, your tongue!

Can you can taste the salt in the air?

Ida Haseu sticks out his tongue.

Ida Haseu

Humm! Yes, I see that one 'can' taste the salt in the air.

Washi Jomo

Also King Haseu, when you move through these areas, there is a bitter taste in the air. I mean, I never knew that a man could 'taste' the stench that he also smell in his nose.

Ida Haseu

I see that there still are many unanswered questions in this life, Bone Man. Maybe you can eliminate more of them for us as we go along on this journey. Never the less, I will return again when we are rested.

Ida Haseu moves through the crowd and disappear among the wet black bodies of the many Slave Captives.

END OF SCENE TWO

Act: 1

Scene: 3

Scene three opens in the same Slave Ship compartment as in scene one and scene two. The Slave Captives continue to experience the same hardships as in scene one and scene two. There are the familiar sounds of waves striking the sides of the Slave Ship, also the traditional sounds of African life continue to dominate the hearing senses. Again the screeching sound of the hatch opening causes the black bodies to move cautiously away from the steps that lead up to the upper deck.

Again, big containers of cooked fish and water each are lowered down into the under deck. Again Ekida and the other women receive and distribute the fish and water, first serving those who are chained in place. The Iboni adults and older children continue to refuse to eat the fish. There is a sobering feeling in the air.

The unchained Slave Captives continue to sit in their tribal groups, rocking back and forth, chanting, sitting in the blood, tears, urine, the vomit and the excrement. The water level is now a few inches higher due to the continued leaking of the patches on the side of the Slave Ship, higher than in scene two, now covering the tops of their feet. Now the sounds of retching and vomiting can be heard above the chants and the traditional sounds of Africa.

The Fresh air again burst into the under deck and the smell of fresh air smells sweet to the senses of the Slave Captives. One of the crewmen are seen peering down into the under deck. The man has a thick cloth covering his nose and mouth, leaving only his eyes uncovered. The crewman is saying something loudly that no one understands. The crewman is holding up his hand, still no one understands.

Crew man

Five men!   1-2-3-4-5. Five men come on up here! Any five!

Holding up five fingers and pointing to the rows of black unchained Slave Captives. The entire wave of unchained Slave Captives move away from the stairs that lead to the upper deck opening.with a muffled voice the crew man continue to shout.

Five!   1-2-3-4-5.   Five men. Five, you dumb bunnies!

Holding up five fingers again, pointing at the rows of Slave Captives. A young woman moves toward the stairs but the crew man stops her. Crew man continues.

No! No! Not you woman! Give me five men! Men! Men! Do you understand me! A man!

Gesturing at his own genitals towards the Slave Captives. Looking around at the Ship's Captain.

They are too scared to come up to me Captain! They are pretending to not understand me.

Captain

If I don't get five out of that hull in five minutes, I want you to go down there and get me five! I- want- five- men- now!

The Crew man starts down the stairs leading into the Slave Ship under deck with the cloth still covering his mouth and nose shielding his senses of smell and taste from the stench of the urine and excrement. Two young Iboni men knowing and excepting their fate, steps forward with lateral, jerky movements. With their movement, the Crew man stops and begin to back his way back up the stairs. The five Iboni men disappear through the hatch door and the door slides slowly closed again. Every dialect can now be heard as each tribal member speak alarm into the ethers, now knowing what the bones has said about those who are taken to the

top side of this Slave Ship. Outraged, Ida Haseu push
his way through the rows of black bodies, motioning
for Ekida and Kuba to follow him to the hiding place
of Washi Jomo, the Bone Thrower.Washi Jomo see the
crowds of Slave Captives all moving in his direction and
he knows that it is King Ida Haseu coming to hear the
remaining words of the sacred bones.

Ida Haseu

Take out your bones Bone Man, and let your bones
speak to us for our own sake.

*The bone Man takes out the old tattered cloth and
removes the bones cautiously. He spreads the cloth out
on one of the few dry places left on the floor level of this
Slave Ship. Washi Jomo again takes the bones into his
thick hands while humming the old Iboni ritual song. He
shakes the bones briskly in his palms, again listening for
the familiar sounds of the bones authority to proceed with
the continuation of their sacred revelations. Again, Washi
Jomo, the Bone Man releases the bones briskly and with
great skill and Science. With a dazzling, spinning effect,
the bones make their contact with the cloth, tumbling,
rolling, and striking each other as they choose their
place on the cloth. Some bones seem to struggle against
each other for dominance in their preparation to say the
words that Washi Jomo, Ida Haseu, and the other Slave
Captives wait desperately to hear.*

*The larger bones are rolling over and trampling over the
smaller bones in order to tell their part of the story first,
not really caring if the smaller bones ever have a chance
to tell their story. As the sacred bones finally comes to
their rest, Washi Jomo painfully studies the layout of
the bones as they lay there throbbing in their intensity.
Washi Jomo looks deeply and carefully at the bones
because he wants to he sure as to their accuracy in case
they have something new to say this time.*

Washi Jomo

Waving his hands over the bones and begin to speak the words as they are reported to him by the larger, more aggressive bones.

O' King, at the end of this long journey, we will all be given new names. We will somehow forget who we are , and, you will no longer be our king.

Looking sadly at King Haseu.

In the years to come we will have forgotten all that you and your fathers has done for our beloved Africa, and much of our history. The old men who knows these truths will die and their wisdom will die with them. Only an remnant will remain. The rivers will all dry up leaving a desolate land and volumes of their wisdom will dry up with them. except what some can remember. The dirt and the heat has no wisdom to impart, leaving the people to wander, searching for an elusive truth.

Ida Haseu studies the bones himself as if trying to see the words that the Bone Man speak, in symbols, or the symbols in words. He is confused, not fully trusting or understanding the power and wisdom of this Bone Man. Feeling deep inside that if by chance any of this is true, this Bone Man is truly underrated. The Bone Man continues.

We will not have time for dance and for play as in our villages. We will not have our women in love and in marriage as we are so accustomed to in our land.

The Bone Man continue to report the story as reported by the larger bones. Now picking up the larger bones again, shaking them again in his palms, listening to them, then throwing them again into the midst of the smaller bones. The larger bones strike the cloth again finding their way to their prescribed places among the smaller bones. Washi Jomo carefully reads the layout of the larger bones again, as they relate to each other

Slave Ship

*and as they relate to the other smaller bones that lay
and wait impatiently to tell their story.*

At the end of this journey we will learn of a new and
more powerful God. This new and powerful God will not
respond to our cry for many, many generations. There
will be a new way that we must learn of at great trial
and error.

*Now Washi Jomo, the Bone Man, turns to the smaller
bones and begin to study their layout.*

At the end of this journey, O' King, we will not build
empires for our selves, but the empires that we build will
be for those who await our arrival. We will do much work
for this people but this people will hate us because of who
we are. The bones does not explain why.

*The Bone Man carefully pick up the smaller bones
again, careful to not disturb the larger bones. He then
bring the smaller bones to his ear again, shaking them
briskly. When he has heard their authority to proceed,
he throws the smaller bones again to the cloth. The
smaller bones land among the larger bones again,
tumbling and striking each other and striking the larger
bones that lay and wait also to hear the words that
the smaller bones prepare to say to the Slave Captives.
Washi Jomo speaking even more confidently.*

At the end of this journey, O' King, we will be held in
bondage by force, by a people who would rather that we
would die like animals than to allow us to roam free in
their own land.

*The Bone Man take a step back, wiping his face and
eyes with his thick hands, then continues to interpret
the small bone layout. Ida Haseu is looking completely
stunned*

We will no longer recognize our land. Neither will we
recognize those of our people who remain there. And our
land will not recognize us. We will try to remember but
we cannot, except for a remnant of us being a chosen few

for the purpose of remembering. The bones so not explain why. At the end of this journey, when we will think that we have done well we will be whipped like animals, and sir, too many of us will die by our necks with a rope. All these things the bones speak clearly to us.

Washi Jomo is angry now, while looking directly into the eyes of Ida Haseu.

There, you said that you wanted to know the truth that the bones have said. Now you know the truth. The bones has spoken to us again.

Ida Haseu

His voice trembling, looking under eyed at Washi Jomo.

Tell... the... bones... to...keep talking!

Washi Jomo

Looking startled!

King Haseu! Sir, these revelations to us by the bones were not revealed to us by your order, nor by my order! This communication does not just work the way that you or I decide that it should. Sir, this is a spiritual matter. We can't just...

Ida Haseu grabs Washi Jomo by his clothing, but releases them when Washi Jomo turned to face him. Again Ida Haseu wade out into the deeper water of confrontation, grasping Washi Jomo tightly by the arm this time. The two men are standing face to face, each in defense of each their own authority. Ida Haseu and Washi Jomo are standing so close in their struggling, that they can each smell the stench of each the others mouth. The smell of their mouths are easily distinguishable from the thick smell of the urine and the excrement that continue to fill the air, the nostrils and the lungs of the Slave Captives. The men struggle more intensively now, neither giving an inch to the other. The men slip and struggle in the ankle deep waste and they both fall, struggling to the floor of the Slave Ship with a splash, rolling and sliding, each imposing their brute strength on the other. Drenched in urine, tears, blood, vomit, sea water and excrement, they both now stand up, compromising but neither man surrendering their believed authority. The entire Slave Captive population are looking on in shock and disbelief, including those who are chained in place, all strain to see and hear.

Washi Jomo

Breathing deeply.

You are our King Chief sir, but sir, you do not understand the...

Ida Haseu

Interrupting

Oh yes, I do understand very clearly. Perhaps it is you who do not understand me, Bone Man. The things that you have said may very well come to pass, but is this 'all that the bones have to say about such an important matter? Are you telling me that the bones have no more to say to us?

Ida Haseu putting his face inches close to Washi Jomo's face again. He continues:

The things that the bones say are hard things for us to hear, but Bone Man, what the bones have said is 'not' enough to cause an entire people aboard this Slave Ship to choose death for their children, for their mothers, and for their fathers. The bones must say more!

Tightly squeezing Washi Jomo's arm again.

Pick... up... the... bones... and... throw them... again... I... command you Mr. Bone Man!

Washi Jomo

Looking startled, taking a step back.

You command me? Did you say that you command me? You may be King but you can not command in the spiritual realm! Have you heard nothing that the bones has said?

Ida Haseu

The bones have not said enough. The bones must say more!

Washi Jomo

The bones has said to us that at the end of this journey, you will no longer be king. That no one will remember you for all that you have done or will do, and yet you command me? I ask you again. Have you heard nothing that the bones has said?

Ida Haseu

Speaking slowly.

Pick- up- the- bones,-Bone- Man- and- throw- them- again. Pick- them- all- up- and- throw- them- all- now. Now, Bone Man!

Washi Jomo

Reluctantly

Alright! Alright! I'll throw the bones again. But I must warn you that there is no guarantee that...

Ida Haseu

Interrupting Washi Jomo.

Just throw the bones, Bone Man now!

Kuba

Trying to intervene on behalf of the Bone Man.

King Haseu, please!

Ida Haseu

Kuba, you must stay silent!

Now speaking to Washi Jomo.

You're not just talking to some mere tribal chief! I am the King Chief of all the Nigeritian people, all over Africa. I am not one to look softly for the truth. Say the truth to me Bone Man! Tell me all that the bones know.

Washi Jomo

Hesitating

Sir! er, sir, may I speak freely to you? Er, in peace of course.

Ida Haseu

Speak Bone Man! Make yourself clear, and stop your stammering, please!

Washi Jomo

Laughing to himself.

You no longer anger me, O' King.
I now have a better understanding of things that I wrongly thought that I fully understood. Things that for so long, I didn't understand at all.

Ida Haseu

What?

Looking around for help from anyone.

What?

Looking around again, completely perplexed. Finally giving in, accepting that he would only delay the bones further by arguing with this Bone Man. Trying to appear calm and Chiefly.

Just what are these things that you now fully understand, Bone Man? Are you having private conversations with the bones while we all sleep?

Washi Jomo

Accommodating

Surly not! I know now that there truly are differences in some men. I know that you truly "are" King and Chief of all of our people. Somehow I know this now, by your unrelenting spirit, just as your father who I have known better than most men. Sir, I am forever indebted to you for my late awakening. Though we all smell badly, you still are distinguished among all of us.

Loud laughter through out the Slave Captive population. Ida Haseu speaks sarcastically to Washi Jomo.

Ida Haseu

I didn't understand what you said Bone Man. Could you please speak louder and clearer, and in all the languages and dialects that you speak? So that all can hear your great words.

They all laugh again.

I still think that you are an angry man, Mr. Bone Man.

Dismissing the Bone Man's sarcasm.

Washi Jomo

No! No! No!

But not willing to give in fully to Ida Haseu. Now continuing.

But, as I was saying, you are not as hard as you would like for us to believe. I believe that you are a gentle man.

Ida Haseu

For God's sake man! I would rather hear what the bones has to say. Say no more.

Washi Jomo

Unwrapping the bones again, and spreading out the old tattered cloth.

What I mean is that your heart is some-what softer for the people than you want us to know.

Ida Haseu again looking impatiently at Washi Jomo.

Ida Haseu

Alright!

Reaching for the bones. Washi Jomo push the hands of Ida Haseu away.

Washi Jomo

Picking up all the bones in his palms, shaking them vigorously at his ear. He stops shaking the bones and speak calmly to Ida Haseu.

You must remember O' King, that you may well have insulted the spirits of these sacred bones. In this, I have no power to intervene for you.

Looking intensively at Ida Haseu.

I must tell you also that, though the bones will not lie to you, they will Not be careful with you either, just because you are king. The bones know who you are. It will be wise for you to remember that you are forcing them from their silence. The bones of the hyena the eagle and the elephant ivory knows no compromise to their privacy.

Ida Haseu stands firm.

Ida Haseu

I am not afraid Bone Man, and you can not enter fear into my mind.

The throngs of Slave Captives tightens the pocket of black bodies around Ida Haseu, Washi Jomo, Kuba, and Ekida.

Washi Jomo

You have said that you want to know further why these Iboni people would rather die than to continue in this low Slave Ship.

Washi Jomo brings the bones down from his ear slowly and release them. The sounds of gasps can be heard all around them. Those who form the pocket wedge around them reset the positions of both their bodies and their minds Still the sounds of children crying can be heard all around them. The familiar sounds of gagging and vomiting is heard again and again.

The sounds of traditional African music continue to fight for it's place in the ears of the Slave Captives, winning some ground then loosing some. Like thunder the bones strike the tattered cloth, tumbling and striking each other angrily, traveling outwardly, until resting at the borders of the full length and full breadth of the cloth. The bones, seeming to desire to report something from every square inch of this cloth, they take their place defensively. Like magic, four small bones make their way to each of the four corners of the cloth like little pawns, protecting the cloth from contamination. Ida Haseu looks around at the bones just as they all come to their halt.

At this moment in time... at this instant, things begin to move in a new slow motion effect on all sides of them. Because of this new slow motion effect, this allows Ida Haseu and Washi Jomo to see each bone somehow three dimensionally, even in their relationship to all the other bones and all the Slave Captives. The entire movement and sounds of the entire Slave Ship now moves in slow motion, rolling and splashing on the waters under them. The Slave Captives lean and move with the movement of the Slave Ship. The Urine and excrement continue to move on the floor of their unconventionally timed voyage Ida Haseu wondered if the drivers of this ship were still driving or if we were all now just adrift, as no sounds has been heard from the top side for some time. Nor has there been any reaction to any of our noises or our out bursts from this under deck. The traditional sounds of Africa continue through out this entire action, but while in slow motion the sounds that we hear are now in a vigorously screwed up effect.

Ida Haseu again reach out to touch the bones and Washi Jomo again push his hands away, Every thing is now like a spinning dream.

Washi Jomo

Washi Jomo, catching his breath, then reports.

The Bones are angry O' King, but they have spoken to you and they will speak to you again. The bones has told these proud African women that these proud African men that they have known, will be brutally brought under subjection by this mans whip that will slash to his bones. The endless rows of White cotton growing out of a black land will cause the proud African mans confusion to know no bounds.

The circle of Slave Captives gasp again and again, some hearing these words for the first time, Washi Jomo continue to report the words that the bones report to him. Washi Jomo places his finger up to his lips and turns in a full circle to Silence everyone who are surrounding them.

Quiet, I say, listen to what the bones say to us!

Ida Haseu grit his teeth hard together, looking into nowhere, but with his ears fully attuned.

Ida Haseu

Continue your report Bone Man!

Washi Jomo continues.by girding up his assertions .and truths.

Washi Jomo

News will come to us in the form of a lie. Many of us will believe this untruth. Though many will be condemned for their unbelief, the truth will come. The truth will come, but it will seem to come with it's real compassion for the one who lied. The ones who lied will dance and laugh at us also. The real truth will never be fully understood for very many generations until there is absolutely no more fear. No more fear.

Ida Haseu head begin to shake, using his now unreliable will power, trying to not visualize any of this that the bones are saying. The reality of the words are so great that they begin to brake through the veil of his conscious mind into the subconscious mind that he is so desperately trying to guard. Maybe this is not the time to hear more.

Ida Haseu

Relenting for compassion sake, and for the sake of those who listen on helplessly and unarmed, cursing the bones.

I have heard enough Bone Man! Say no more! Your words has poisoned my ears, and the ears of all of your countrymen. Maybe this is not the time to hear more! God damn these bones and God damn you Bone Man!

Washi Jomo

You do not anger me Ida Haseu, but be careful because the bones knows everything that we do not know. You said that you wanted to know the whole truth. You said that you were not afraid to know the truth. Now you curse the bones, and you curse me, because I report the truth? The bones will continue to speak to us whether we will hear them or not. The words will lie in the ethers if they are ever needed by any of those who come after us.

Ida Haseu

I guess I don't have the power to stop you. It seems that you and your bones have all the power, So I guess you should continue!

Washi Jomo

Girding up his assertions again and continues his report.

These lies that the bones speak of will cause fear and confusion in our minds, for too many generations and causing us to turn against each other viciously during this slavery time, and we will remain there in this spirit until there is absolutely no more fear. No more fear!

Looking hard, studying the total layout of the bones.

Many who would not die, will die, for no other purpose than fear. Not enough people will care, because of their own fears. No one will long for us who do not witness the truth of our fears. Some will run from this fear because of they who will laugh when we who remembers, say that our fathers were Kings and our mothers were Queens. They will all laugh when there is nothing funny. We will try again and again to tell them that our fathers are Kings and our Mothers are Queens and they will laugh again when there is nothing funny.

Ida Haseu

My God! Oh my God! This whole evil thing is contrived!

Ida Haseu is in a daze. Washi Jomo continues.

Washi Jomo

We will believe the truth for as long as we can, but the cotton, and the whip, will drive us to unbelief in ourselves, and in our truth, except for a remnant of us. Many will die not knowing the truth or knowing the lie.

Ida Haseu

Relenting.

Ok! Ok! That's enough Bone Man!

Washi Jomo

This is not all that the bones say. There is more, O' King. The bones say to these proud African men, that the proud African women whom they have known will again and again be forced to ware rags on their bodies for clothing, hiding their beauty that we say is ours. Other men who laugh at us, will claim our pleasures for themselves causing us to confuse love with hate and hate with love, then mock us as they dance in their denials. This is what the bones say to us O' King. There will be no mercy.

Ida Haseu continues to feel a deep depression slowly creeping upon his mind, body, and spirit. The Bone Man continues the verbal and spiritual assault upon him and his fellow Slave Captives. Washi Jomo feels no remorse in relating the words of the bones, as it is Ida Haseu who is forcing the reluctant bones out of their spiritual silence. The Bone Man continues.

The bones say to the proud African men, that the proud African women whom they have known will also be subject to the foul smelling bed huts set up by this man to hide his deeds with her and to brake her spirit for a time until the veil is removed from her eyes and mind.

Ida Haseu

I have heard enough Bone Man. I understand now why the Iboni people has chosen death over life in this thing of slavery. You have no need to say anything more.

Ida Haseu opens his mouth and stick out his tongue and again he can taste salt and the stale, rank, musk of the sweating bodies of the Slave Captives. Somehow he can taste the urine, the excrement and the other foul smells in the air of the Slave Ship under deck. The over whelming influence of the bobbing movements of this Slave Ship is apparent more and more as time goes on and retching and. vomiting is heard over and over again all around them in the Slave Ship.

Ida Haseu's mind is traveling back to the many times that he has spoken to the young children of the villages to avoid the serpents, and how the serpent can sample the air and taste ones presence and movement in much the same way that he can now taste the fear in the air as the Bone Man speak.

Washi Jomo

Still looking at the bones while speaking to Ida Haseu. The slow motion effect continues in the minds and being of all the riders.

King Haseu, this Slave Ship that we ride upon has a name.

Ida Haseu

Looking startled!

What? What did you say?

Washi Jomo

Yes! I am saying to you that this Slave Ship is named "The High Truth" .

Ida Haseu

less astounded.

Well... I guess one must call a Slave Ship by some name to justify their Great lie.

Washi Jomo

Bringing his face closer to Ida Haseu's face.

O' King! There are as we speak almost one hundred Slave Ships such as this High Truth Slave Ship, on these waters at this same hour.

Ida Haseu

Say no more Bone Man! You have said enough! I now understand the motivation of the Iboni people, and why they would choose death. I do not agree with their choice but I understand them better.

Washi Jomo

Continuing defiantly.

Yes, we are captured and maybe we have no way out.

The magnitude of this entire voyage and the consequences weighs squarely and heavily on the mind, shoulders, and spirit of Ida Haseu, and even increasingly on Washi Jomo. Consequences that match the weights that has long weighed heavily on the shoulders and minds of the Iboni people.

Ida Haseu looks around at the many Slave Captives forming the throbbing pocket of black bodies around them. He looks up and over this pocket of black bodies, at those who are chained in place at a distance all around the walls of this Slave Ship. The action is no longer just moving in slow motion. Somehow the action on this Slave Ship is moving in an erratic, staccato-blur, movement. Speeding up and slowing down at fractured intervals, seemingly unopposed by those who are riding on this Slave Ship, 'High Truth'.The traditional sounds of Africa continue, though they are fragmented. Ida Haseu is trying to push all that he has heard out of his mind, at least temporarily , trying to concentrate while searching for the right place to stand in the urine and excrement. Even the most fragmented parts of his mind brake again into even smaller more minute pieces. The sharp pieces are causing unbearable pain in his head like which he has never experienced before.

The chanting starts up again, more intensively now as the Slave Captives make their way back to their place, forming the rows and rows of black bodies. The tribes now all chant in harmonic unison, each seeming to know the harmonic plans of the others who join in the chants.

Male Chanters

In deep resonant voices.

Oooooo- mmmlaaa- laaa- la- la- la- ma- saaaaah- awash- Hooomp.

Ummm- mmmm- oooohh- ummmm- maaaa- Huuummp.

Female Chanters

In a familiar high pitched tone that travel from the tongues of the female Slave Captives, are received with pride, piercing and soothing every ear and every spirit, their voices explode also.

Li- li- li- li- li- li- li- li- li- li- li- li- li- li- li- li- li- li- li- li- li- li- li- li- li.

Li- li- li- li- li- li- li- li- li- li- li- li- li- li- li- li- li- li- li-
li- li- li.

*The sounds of chanting mix with the traditional sounds
of Africa and the rhythmic drum sounds, and is soothing
to all of the Slave Captives. The chanting goes back and
forth from the male chanters to the female chanters in
a call and response order. Ida Haseu begin to pick up
his feet in a slow, walking- in- place- manner, causing
ripples in the ankle deep waste. He begin also to slide
his feet in a more rhythmic and more deliberate motion
as though dancing. Hundreds of voices sing, hundreds
of eyes see and hundreds of chained in place minds
visualize until the entire scene blend into one motion.
The Slave Captives chant, watching Ida Haseu's every
movement, aligning their voices and their rhythms
with his steps. The voices, in song, begin to call for Ida
Haseu to dance the traditional 'dance that symbolizes
victory and success over all things that threaten the well
being and existence of the African people and even the
continent of Africa.*

Voices

Haseu! Dancer!-Haseu! Dancer!-Haseu! Dancer!-
Haseu! Dancer!-Haseu! Dancer!-Haseu! Dancer!-Haseu!
Dancer!

*Ida Haseu now begin to turn and dance faster and faster,
writhing faster and faster, splashing and splashing in
the urine and the excrement that has become so much
a part of their lives. The voices continue.*

Haseu! Dancer!-Haseu! Dancer!-Haseu! Dancer!-
Haseu! Dancer!-Haseu! Dancer!-Haseu! Dancer!-Haseu!
Dancer!

*Ida Haseu dances faster and faster in great expression.
Faster and faster, moving his legs, feet and arms
symbolizing victory in all of his important endeavors.
Finally Ida Haseu collapses from exhaustion into
the sweating wall of black Slave Captives. The Slave*

Captives that can see their Kings face, all collectively pretend to not see the tears falling like rain from the eyes of their King. The wall of Slave Captives hold up their king from falling into the urine and excrement. Again the sweating black bodies part, as Kuba and Ekida guides the limp person of Ida Haseu towards the front of the Slave Ship, 'The High Truth' Slowly coming back to his full consciousness Ida Haseu is without strength and without words. But he does now remembers the reason why he is so overwhelmed.

Ida Haseu

There is to much pain in the things to come. The bones has spoken and my heart goes out to my people, to the beautiful, peaceful people of Africa.

Ida Haseu finds Washi Jomo with his eyes, while focusing over the waves and waves of sweating black bodies. Fixing his eyes upon Washi Jomo, blocking out all the chanting voices. Standing paralyzed, absorbing the damage that is being done to him by all the images flooding his mind and being . Overwhelmed by Images of things to come. Images too graphic to hold in his mind for more than a moment at a time. There are higher, more intense moments. Looking at Ekida, who is crying louder now. Ida Haseu touches Ekida's shoulder, speaking to her in a low voice.

Our people are suffering so much pain. So much pain. I'm sorry to be so helpless.

Ekida

Looking at Ida Haseu through crying eyes, struggling with her composure.

I too am sorry for my people 'and' for crying so much. I really am a much stronger woman than it might seem. I guess I must have heard much more than I was prepared to hear about our hope and our future. We truly need for

God to be with us, because there is nothing that we can do for ourselves except ride this Slave Ship and pray.

Ida Haseu

Providing strength for Ekida.

Oh yes, we all know that you are a strong woman Ekida. You do not have to explain or justify your emotions to me. I have no doubt about your strength as a woman and as a soldier. You are leading us now, as we defend your honor. You are our woman, as are all women that are here, and as you defend yourselves, we defend you also. Cry if you must, but you must not stop marching. A victory for us on this Slave Ship is a victory for all of our people, now and forever.

Ida Haseu wipes Ekida's tears with his hands, calming her and simulating a crown of gold on her head. The Slave Captives are falling asleep in their places, exhausted from the strain of the past few hours. There is near total silence now on this Slave Ship, except for the sounds of African drums and the traditional sounds from the distant shores of Africa. The sounds of the giant waves continue to strike the side of the Slave Ship. Ekida fall asleep also while she embrace Ida Haseu. He gently lay her down in the blood, sweat, urine and excrement without waking her. Ida Haseu looks around and see that there seem to be no one awake but he himself. Perhaps every Slave Captives on this Slave Ship just pretending to be asleep. How else can everyone be asleep at the same time. He runs his tired fingers through his graying hair, pondering the right things to do. He walks slowly around the sleeping bodies trying to not Wake anyone. Standing with his back to the wall of the Slave Ship, he is wondering again how everyone can fall asleep at the same time. He turn to what he believe to be the east to ask the creator for guidance. While getting down on his knees in the waste to pray he could see that the water level in the Slave Ship is rising fast. Water is leaking into the Slave Ship

*even faster now from a badly leaking patch that he
had not seen. While inspecting the badly leaking patch
for several moments Ida Haseu can hear the sounds
of someone walking, splashing in the waste behind
him. It is young Kuba approaching him with something
wrapped in a cloth, handing it to Ida Haseu.*

Kuba

Chief Ida Haseu, this is for you. Maybe this will help
you to make the decisions that lie at the edges of your
mind.

*Ida Haseu received the clothed instrument, looking
conversely at it with raised eye brows. He removed the
cloth to find that this Iboni warrior, Kuba has delivered
to him some kind of striking instrument. Kuba continues.
Looking deep into the eyes of Ida Haseu.*

I am sorry to startle you O' King, one of the Iboni
who are chained in place had found this instrument
three days ago in the wall of this slave ship. We have
difficultly waited for the proper time in which to present
this instrument to you. Our question to you though from
this Iboni people is this: Are you the right person that we
should present such an instrument to?

Ida Haseu

Somehow I knew that you would be here at this
time.

Sarcastically.

Somehow I knew that you would be here to insure
that I fulfill and complete the office that I hold.

*Looking around, Ida Haseu is startled to see that Kuba
is no longer there.*

*He is gone back to his place, joining those who pretends
to be asleep. Ida Haseu looks at the badly leaking patch,
then looks at the striking instrument. He sit down by the*

patch, sitting in the urine, the vomit, and the excrement undeterred. Again Ida Haseu look around at the faces. The faces of the Slave Captives glow, reflecting against each other the light and shadow of their souls and spirits. Each soul finding their own reality, reflecting each their entire physical and spiritual images up, down, and to each side of themselves. Filling every inch of space available in this moment of eternal reality.

For the Slave Captives, this is somehow the fullness of time.
Expanding, moving the limits of their potential love.
Expanding, moving the limits of their potential valor.
Expanding, moving the limits of their potential peace.
Expanding, moving the limits of their potential joy.
Expanding, moving the limits of their potential hope.
Expanding, moving the limits of their potential trust.
Expanding, moving the limits of their potential hate.
Expanding, moving the limits of their potential capacity.
Expanding, moving the limits of their potential endurance.

Encountering these gifts genetically within the spirits and souls of their royal selves.

Embracing them all for a time then leaving them alone to ferment, and seethe in the unattended ethers.

Ida Haseu

Clutching the instrument with his entire being, pushing it away from himself then bringing it back to himself again.

Looking, but not really seeing those Slave Captives that pretend to be asleep.

Oh God, If I could just see the moon, the sun, and the stars again.

Brushing the instrument as though brushing away grime from a treasure.dug and mined from the souls of a deflated Iboni people. The painful sight of his country men in total pain pierces the left brain lobe of Ida Haseu again and again. The pain and the sorrow is real in his life and there is nothing that he or anyone else can do about it. He is straining in his mind to remember who he really is, trying to remember his name. Trying to remember some pleasant moment that he has shared with his lovely wife, whom he has not spoken of and whom he has forced himself to not confront mentally during this entire voyage He is not trying to understand. He is not trying to justify. Finally Ida Haseu can recall the memories that he is searching for. Words are now escape freely from their prison in his mind exiting his mouth involuntarily, as though to unseen listeners.

Ida Haseu who once looked tall, confident, elegant and commanding in his own space and around all others, now feel small and insignificant, having shrunk under the pressure of knowing too many devastating future events due to occur in their lives.

The thick air that the Slave Captives all breathe now has a wet bitter taste to it, and the thickness of it clings to their tongues and their skin, causing condensation on the walls of their minds and spirits. Ida Haseu begin to hum another old traditional African Victory song.

Aiiii aaa nanana na na waaaaa mummm!
Aiiii aaa nanana na na waaaaa mummm!

Like an angel of God, a little Iboni girl of about 7 years of age, get up rubbing sleep from her eyes.

She join Ida Haseu in humming this old traditional African Victory song.

Aiiii aaa nanana na na waaaaa mummm!
Aiiii aaa nanana na na waaaaa mummm!

John H.Hall

The little Iboni girl walk slowly over to where Ida Haseu is sitting in the urine, blood, tears, vomit, excrement and sea water hacking away at the already violently leaking patch on the side of the slave ship. The little girl begin to pull away the splinters and chipped pieces from the leaking patch with her little hands. Ida Haseu is now hacking and hacking with all his strength. No one has heard anything, except this one little girl. Maybe the Captors or the Slave Ship's crew can hear the loud hacking sounds or maybe not. Maybe the captors and Slave Ship's crew had heard the sounds of loud singing, or maybe not. Maybe the captors and Slave Ship's crew can hear the loud chanting mixed with the traditional sounds of Africa and the African drum rhythms and all the other the sounds, or maybe not.

Maybe the captors and the Slave Ship's crew can feel the sheer inevitability and the determination of all of their fate, or maybe not.

Maybe the captors and the Slave Ship's crew can feel the sheer determination of the Slave Captives will to be free, or maybe not.

Maybe the captors and the Slave Ship's crew has been over come by the overwhelming smell of the urine, the vomit, and the excrement, or maybe not.

Maybe the captors and the Slave Ship's crew can feel the spirits of the Slave Captives moving below them, or maybe not.

Never the less,, Ida Haseu and this little Iboni girl child continue to sing, hack and pull away the splintered pieces of the leaking patch. This badly leaking patch is the only thing that stand between the Iboni Slave Captives and their perceived freedom.

Without warning, lightning seems to strike this Slave Ship at the point of the leaking patch. Great walls of water burst through the patch, violating what is left

56

of the integrity and buoyancy of this once rock solid Slave Ship, causing a shift in it's responsibilities of delivery and it's abilities of navigation. Sounds louder that thunder, roars over and over again. The thunderous sound are louder perhaps than has ever been heard by man or beast. Yet it continues to inflict itself on this helpless people who ride this, now doomed, Slave Ship. The Slave Ship, bucking with great force, leaning far on it's left side, then bucking with even greater force, leaning far on it's right side. The captors and the ship's crew on the top side of the Slave Ship can be heard cursing, using great obscenities. The sounds of heavy objects falling, takes up the rest of the space in their brains capacity that is allotted for hearing loud sounds. Nothing greater, in terms of loud sounds can be heard at this time.

The introduction of such great volumes of water into the hull of the Slave Ship so quickly is causing the vessel to loose is buoyancy at a faster rate than can even be imagined. Water is everywhere! Water is everywhere! Water is everywhere! The sheer brute force of the inexhaustible water and the erratic movement of this Slave Ship throws bodies against bodies, mingling those Slave Captives who are unchained, with those Slave Captives who are chained in place. The blood, urine, tears, sweat, vomit, sea water and excrement is now at large, moving freely within the hull of this Slave Ship on all levels.

The Slave Ship continues to bucks again and again, leaning far on each side while the sounds of violent crashes can be heard over and over again.

Throwing our drowning bodies!
Throwing our drowning peace!
Throwing our drowning spirituality!
Throwing our drowning knowledge!
Throwing our drowning hope!
Throwing our drowning love!
Throwing our drowning dreams!

Throwing our drowning trust!
Throwing our drowning nationality!
Throwing our drowning freedom!
Throwing our drowning understanding!
Throwing our drowning family!
Throwing our drowning power!
Throwing our drowning lives!
Throwing our drowning culture!
Throwing our drowning honesty!
Throwing our drowning experiences!
Throwing our drowning smiles!
Throwing our drowning wisdom!
Throwing our drowning marriages!
Throwing our drowning motherhood!
Throwing our drowning fatherhood!

Throwing our drowning Royalty, firmly up against the walls of this sinking Slave Ship, Yet, the Slave Captives say nothing, they just ride their fate with great unparalleled dignity. What now seems like the end of the world is taking place on this very Slave Ship as we speak! Loud screaming can be heard over and over again on the top deck. Ida Haseu struggle to square his shoulders, moving completely in front of the Iboni girl child, to absorb the continuing blast of waters, but there is no safe place. There is no place to hide. Ida Haseu can do nothing to stop the effect of the rushing and rising waters, no one can. The patch now gives in completely, bursting with a loud deafening bang, filling the Slave Ship completely with stale tasting, salty tasting, fishy tasting, urine and excrement tasting waters in their mouths and noses. Ida Haseu's thoughts flash again to the top side crew. He can hear them now screaming over and over again. The black bodies of the Slave Captives continue to mingle and wash away from their places and back again, as more and more bodies are now floating. Ida Haseu can see Washi Jomo out of the corners of his eyes going under the waters of death and coming up again and again. Washi Jomo offers no resistance. He just passively allow the waters to carry him where ever they will. Ida Haseu holds his breath for a few seconds,

then release his breath under the water. He can hear
the air from his lungs escaping causing the bubbles that
flee upward, to selfishly, save themselves. The bubbles
seem to burst in slow motion, not really caring if they
burst now or at a later time, as there is no demand on
their time. Through the murky waters Ida Haseu sees
Ekida and Kuba float by. They both look asleep and
both are holding each others arms.

Somehow everything seems so much clearer now. Ida
Haseu can visualize the moon shining long on the waters
of death. The Slave Ship begin to brake into several
pieces. No one is trying to escape. No one is trying to
help anyone else to survive. The dead and the living are
just riding and riding, each traversing time and space
simultaneously. In Ida Haseu's dying thoughts...

Ida Haseu

Be it known! Be it known, that I have not abandoned
my people, and have not abandoned my post. I have
stayed faithful to our customs and our beliefs.

The bones has said to me that those who survive these
voyages are not necessarily those who are the strongest
of us, as it is so often said. Those who survive this middle
passage and manage to reach the western world are not
the most fit of us, but those who refuse to go are they.
Those who refuse to go at all costs are they!

The bones said to me that those who ride the thousands
of Slave Ships after us, and arrive should look around
themselves and when you are standing among each
other... Ask your brothers keeper where are the numbers
of men who would be here? Those who are left alone in
the waters of death.

Honor is for the families of those who refused to go?

Where are the numbers of our men, women and
children who would have been be, but are not?

Where are the families of us who would be, but
cannot?

Who will represent the families of us who are not in our midst?

Who will inquire on behalf of those who died the deaths of soldiers before they could receive the promise of their freedoms?

Who will bring them to us? Who will be appointed to bring them?

As my spirit leaves my body, I feel a hunger for my God!

As my spirit leaves my body, the rushing waters say to me that it is too late to resend decisions made here.

As my spirit leaves my body, I concede that I will be judged by some as being one who too, has committed an atrocity, to satisfy the thirst of the Iboni.

To you I say that, you do not ride upon this Slave Ship, yet! Subject to this inhuman treatments, yet! Subject to the smells of life upon this Slave Ship, and middle passage, yet.

As my spirit leaves my body I make no excuses for my acts. I do not apologize for my graphic ending of our plight. Intrinsic in the reality of slavery is the very definition of explicitness. For my acts I do not apologize.

Some who are dead continue even in death to hold on
to the broken pieces of this Slave Ship. Their hands grip
as in life.

As my spirit leaves my body, I say to you God bless Africa! Please take us with you my God! Take us with you today! Take us back to our beloved Africa! Please God, bless the African....

END OF PLAY

BURNT OFFERING ©
A Tower Of Shadow

THE PLAY

BY

JOHN H. HALL

CAST OF CHARACTERS

Weeda

Omas

Rabbit

Tweety

Master Fields

Overseer Lester Smith

Lt. Downs

Freedom Woman

Slave Driver 1

Slave Driver 2

Slave Driver 3

Slave Woman 1

Slave Woman 2

Slave Catcher 1

Slave Catcher 2

Time: In the late spring, during the highest point of Slavery in the United States of America.

Place: In the deep southern United States: The Fields Plantation.

ACT: 1

SCENE: 1

Scene one opens in the front porch area of an old Slave Cabin. Two elderly Slave Women are sitting on the steps of the porch laughing and talking with Weeda and Omas. Weeda is sitting on the porch rocking and shelling peas into a small pot. Omas is standing on the ground on the other side of the porch, leaning against a chopping hoe. Omas is telling tall tales as the action starts and they are all laughing. Weeda looks up and see Master Fields riding up on his horse. He has another young man with him that is dressed like him, in the same type of confederate uniform. The younger mans uniform looks dusty also, but not quite as worn as the uniform that Master Fields wear. The laughing stops abruptly. Weeda wipes her face with her apron and stands up. She then motions to the other Slave Women to go. Omas stays.

Weeda

You all go on your way and find something to do.

Motioning to the Slave women again.

It looks like the Master is here to talk. And, he has got someone else with him this time. Hummph, I wonder what he wants around here now.

The two Slave Women exit quickly. Weeda sits back down and lean back in her rocking chair and begin to rock slowly back and forth, never taking her eyes off the

*young man with Master Fields. Master Fields and the
other Confederate officer dismount from their horses.
They walk slowly up to the porch, observing every thing,
including the two women who exited. Master Fields,
looking under eyed at Weeda and Omas , not speaking
immediately. Finally Master fields take off his hat and
begin to knock the dust from his Confederate uniform.*

Weeda

*Continuing to shell peas while looking up at Master
Fields, and the other Confederate officer.*

Good morning Master Fields, and you sir. How are you
all this nice morning?   How is the war coming along? I
hope we are winning. Master Fields I don't see why these
old blue coats don't just leave us alone. We can hear all
that shooting. Some times all night long.

Master Fields

*After a long silence, the Master speaks, nodding his
head in a speaking gesture.*

We are winning, rightly so! But that's not what I came
to talk to you and Omas about. I've only been gone for a
few days now, and all hell done broke loose on this farm.
I want to know from you and omas just what's been going
on around here in these parts. You all promised me that
you would keep an eye out for me and let me know if you
see or hear anything. Or maybe I should be asking you
all If you have been here all day and night long or are
you all trying to run off too, as old as you are.

Weeda

With one hand on her hip.

Now just where are we going to go Master Fields? You
know that we can't leave this place. If we did the Slave

Catchers would be all over us as soon as we get to that clearing.

Pointing to clearing.

Master Fields

Taking out his pipe, lights it, putting the rest of the pipe tobacco on the end of the porch to tempt Omas. Omas just looks at the tobacco, but does not touch it.

Weeda, Omas, I'm hearing that there is some more funny things going on in these parts, and here about. I mean right now, it's too much moving around by this Slave Population.Run-a-ways every day from almost every farm.

No one from this farm lately, but there is talk about meetings and such as that. That under-ground Slave stealing, old devil of a woman is close to these parts again. Are you all telling me that you haven't heard anything about that?

Weeda and Omas are looking at each other and then at Master Fields in complete disbelief at his questions. Master Fields continues.

All the Slaves from the other farms are acting funny. We don't know what's on their minds. And you're telling me that you haven't heard anything about this at all??

Weeda

Looking around at Omas who shakes his head and then looks down at the ground.

No sir, Mr. Fields we haven't heard a thing about this. We haven't heard any talk like that. This just what we do every day, Master. We are the last ones to hear anything that is bad like this is. We only know things if you tell us Master. We don't know nothing about no devil woman. I pray to God for you to believe us Master Fields, were telling you the truth.

Master Fields

Ahhh, I don't believe that for one minute Weeda.

Taking back the tobacco that he had used to tempt Omas with.

Now Weeda, you and Omas. I'm letting you and the rest of them live on here with me like I promised my papa that I would when he was living. Now I don't want you all to mistake me. Do you hear me?

Master Fields is looking deadly serious. The young Confederate officer has been quiet for the whole time, just observing the whole conversation. He now takes his hat off and dusts off his Confederate uniform, and wipes his face with a rag. Now Weeda can clearly see the black stare of this young Confederate officer. Lt. Downs has the facial look and such a lean body look of a real snake. He has the presence of someone who was there, but was not really there.This young officer has not spoken up to this point but he has a fearsome way of engulfing the entire air supply and the entire controversial situation that has been spent, tasting it, sampling the used air and the unresolved controversy, searching them for lies and deception as would a snake. The young Confederate officer whispers something into the ear of Master Fields. They both look at Weeda then Omas. Master Fields touches the young officer on his shoulder, pushing him towards Omas, while they both are still looking at him.

Master Fields

Omas, go with Lt. Downs around to the back of the shack. Go on with him!

Motioning to Omas.

Omas

Omas takes a step backward looking around at Weeda as though pleading for her to do something or say something to Master Fields for him. But Omas has been in this type of situation many times before. Omas knows that this is a road that he must travel alone. Omas also knows that survival must be his only goal.

Yes sir, I'm going on, Master Fields.

Weeda

Looking at Master Fields with a pleading look.

Now Master Fields! We are old folks. Omas and me is always right here. We can't do no harm to you. You are always good to us and we just love you for it.

Master Fields

I said go on with him Omas! Go on now! Lt. Downs is a good man, he just wants to build more honesty and truth with you slavery people.

Lt. Downs

Sticking out his tongue, tasting the air all around Omas and this Slave cabin environment.

So, you are Omas! I've heard quite a lot about you, mostly about you and your young years on this farm. Yes, I've heard that you were quite a spark in your younger days. Is that right or wrong?

Seeing that Omas is a little nervous.

Put that chopping hoe down Omas, you ain't chopping nothing right now.

Lt. Downs takes Omas by his arm and leads him around to the back of the Slave cabin, pushing him in his back while walking behind him.

First of all, I want to let you know that I don't care much of anything about none of you Slavery blacks folks. And not only that, I believe that you folks here are too old to work or to help Colonel Fields in any way at all. Why he keep you all on her, I don't know.

But all in all, that's the Colonel's decision, not mine. But I need to let you know before hand that my business with you is rooted in absolute truth. I hope that you know what truth is.

Lt. Downs pulls his sword from it's sheath and points it directly at front of Omas's neck for a long moment, finally speaking to Omas again.

I don't mind telling you black Omas, that it would give me the greatest pleasure to just cut your neck off right here and right now.That way I won't have to hear your lies.

Lt. Downs returns his sword to it's sheath believing that he has at least partially received his desired result. Omas exhales loudly, pushing air from deep within lungs, his voice creating grunting, vibrating, trembling sounds.

Lt. Downs, stepping forward towards Omas while secretly breathing in the air that has been just breathed out by Omas.He begin pushing Omas on each shoulder backward, causing him to stumble backward, falling and getting back up again, only for Lt. Downs to push him back down again and again. Each time Omas gets back up again and stands up straight. Lt. Downs then puts both hands around Omas's neck and begin to choke and shake him violently. Omas coughs and gags deeply while carefully avoiding eye contact with the young Lt. Downs. Lt. Downs let go of Omas's neck, pushing him hard to the ground again. Lt. Downs continues:

Now, tell me what you know about this Freedom Women. Have she been around here? Don't make me have to cut out your tongue for lying. I'm asking you one more time. Have- that- Freedom- Woman- been- around- here? Don't you lie to me Omas!

Omas

Coughs again, feeling increasingly unstable. Struggles to get up to a standing position again.

Why are you so mad at me Master? We haven't done anything. And we sure haven't seen or heard nothing about no Freedom Woman.

Lt. Downs

Stop it! Stop it! Stop your lies! I don't believe that crap for one minute. I know that she has been in these part, I can feel it in my bones! Get down! Get down on your knees again.

Lt. Downs takes out his long Confederate revolver and points it an inch from Omas's head and quickly pulls back the trigger. I'm running out of patience with you old man. Omas struggles his way down to his knees again, avoiding eye contact with the snake that he sees inside the person of this young Confederate officer.

I could kill you right now and no one will even care. If I kill you no one will even question me about it. Or maybe you want me to 'kill' your old woman or your boy?

Omas

Looks up sharply.

Master, my woman and my boy don't know nothing about any of this Freedom Woman talk. We just don't know nothing at all. Please believe us Master.

Lt. Downs

Don't you play that darkie game with me boy. Don't you play hard of hearing with me! Don't you play dumb with me!

Striking Omas across the side of his head with his Confederate revolver, discharging a huge round into the ground that kicks up dirt a foot high.

I said that I will kill every last one of you darkies right here, now. Are you doubting me? Do you think that I've got the time and the desire to stand here and yack with you people about this.

At the sound of the revolver discharging, Weeda struggles to free her self from the grip of Master fields, trying to run to the back of the house. Master fields grabbs Weeda's arm with a firmer grip, digging his finger nails deep into her skin, as she struggles to go to Omas.

Master Fields

The Lt. Is just getting Omas's attention. I told you that Lt. Downs just wants to build more honesty and trust with you Slavery people. Don't worry about Omas. I'm talking to you around here!

Weeda is trying to pull away from Master Fields, screaming loudly.

Look at me! Look at me, Weeda. I will ask you again. Have any of you heard anything about this so called Devil Woman, this Freedom woman?

Weeda

No sir, Master! No sir, Master! I swear Master Fields, we haven't heard anything. Please Master Fields, don't do us this way. Omas is all that I've got in the world, him and Rabbit.

Master Fields

I don't care about none of that. I'm telling you that this Freedom Woman is coming into these parts disrupting our way. We aim to stop her! And we will stop her, with your help or not.

Omas

Holding his head, his ragged shirt is soaked with blood. Speaking to Lt. Downs.

Please Master! Have mercy on us! We haven't done anything, and we don't know anything.

Lt. Downs

Omas, If I ever hear your name again, out of anyone's mouth, that isn't right by Colonel Fields, I'll be coming back for you! And when I leave again, it's not going to be any one left alive in this Slave Camp but me and your Master Fields. Do you understand me old man?

Lt. Downs slowly walks around behind Omas. Pointing at the back wall of the Slave cabin.

Look at the wall!

Lt. Downs took a step backward and lunged forward with a vicious kick that lands in the seat of Omas's behind that kicks old Omas viciously to the ground. Omas couldn't get up from the ground with all of his strength. Lt. Downs leaves Omas on the ground and starts back to the front of the cabin. Looking back at omas struggling to get up, Lt. Downs goes back and grabs Omas by the back of the neck, forcing him up and leading him back to the front of the cabin where Master Fields continues to interrogate Weeda.

Master Fields

Standing Weeda and Omas up in front of him and Lt. Downs.

I don't want you all to mistake me! You two are too old to work for me now, and you aren't any good to me at all, and you all are too old for me to sell, because no one else wants you.

Weeda

Avoiding eye contact with Master Fields and Lt. Downs. Out of the corners of her eyes she can see little Rabbit standing in the shadows of the tree line.

We understand you Master Fields. We are bound to you. You know that we won't do nothing like mistake you.

Weeda is happy inside because Omas is still alive.

We know that you've been good to me and the others. You are all that me and we has got in the whole world, except little Rabbit and the little garden that you are kind enough to let us work.

Omas

Omas, clearing up his throat and standing up strait.

We haven't seen nothing funny going on around here Master Fields. And we sure haven't heard no talk about no Devil Woman. If we did we would surly tell you first thing. That's just those trouble makers starting that kind of talk.

Weeda

That's right Master, I don't know why folks start that kind of talk. They go and get you all worked up for nothing. Master, you ought to know that me and Omas ain't going to keep nothing from you that we know about.

Lt. Downs goes to get the horses that has walked away grazing.

Master Fields

Alright, I'm trying to believe you all, but I want you to keep your eyes open and let me know everything that you hear about also

Looking around.

Oh yes, where is your boy Rabbit?

Weeda

Rabbit went out to the stream to tote water for the washer women with the other boys, just like you told him to do, Master. You know that Rabbit is always going to do right by you too Master.

Master Fields

Turning to leave.

All right then, you all had better not let me down. Just keep your eyes open around here and let me know if you see or hear anything. Do you understand? Oh, and by the way, Omas, I want you to take your boy Rabbit up to the Overseer's quarters and let Overseer Smith look at him to see if he can help me with some field work yet. Do you hear me Omas?

Omas

Clearing up his throat and looking at weeda.

Yes sir Master. I hear you Master Fields.

Master Fields and Lt. Downs mount their horses to exit. Neither of the men speak as they ride off. Their horses are creating a huge dust cloud behind them in the thin soil. The dust cloud seems to validate them by respectfully following them in all of their believed glory and believed supremacy.

END OF SCENE ONE

Act: 1

Scene: 2

Omas could not walk or stand for two days after his encounter with Master Fields and Lt. Downs. Omas was weak in his body, but he has been in this position many times before in his early years on this farm. He knew that his body would eventually heal and he knew also that he could not complain. Weeda nursed Omas back to health as quickly as she possibly could so that the farm Overseer would not come looking for him. She also needed to be sure that Rabbits first encounter with the farm Overseer did not end in disaster. Weeda and Omas both knew that they had won in this brutal encounter with the Master Fields and Lt. Downs.

It is early evening and the support Slaves to the Field workers are arriving at the yard and are putting away equipment that is not in use for the rest of the day. There is a great deal of movement in and around the Slave camp. One Slave Driver is in the Overseer's quarters suffering from a snake bite injury.

Scene two opens with Omas and Rabbit knocking at the door of the Plantation Overseer's quarters.

Slave Driver 1

Limping on an ailing leg, meeting Omas and Rabbit at the door.

If you all are looking for Overseer Smith, he is not hear yet, but come on in here and state your business. Maybe I can help you in your Slavery needs. Ha- Ha- Ha- Ha- Ha.

Omas and Rabbit steps into the room of the Overseer's quarters.

Ok, now you're letting mosquitoes in here! Close the door! Close that door quick!

Omas closes the door quickly. He and Rabbit just stands there at attention.looking down at the floor, avoiding eye contact with the Slave Driver.

That's right, you all just stand right there. Right where you are. Overseer Smith will be here directly.

At that instant the screen door flings open hard. The door is almost torn from it's hinges. Overseer Lester Smith burst into the doorway with two other Slave Drivers along with him. They are talking loud and laughing. Together with the other Slave Drivers they all fill the room. There is hardly enough room for Omas and Rabbit to stand, despite their meekness. Omas and Rabbit both are highly intimidated by being in such close quarters with the Overseer and the Slave Drivers. Omas's only desire at this time is to help Rabbit to survive this first real, personal, close encounter with the Overseer and the Slave Drivers.

Overseer Smith

Speaking to Slave Driver 1.

How is that leg?

Slave Driver 1

Shaking his leg.

Oh, I think I'll live. But I can't say as much for the snake involved.

They all laugh, except Omas and Rabbit.

Ha- Ha- Ha- Ha- Ha- Ha- Ha.

Slave Driver 2

I told Black Tom that I was going to make him bite the snake's head off.

John H.Hall

They all laugh again.

Ha- Ha- Ha- Ha- Ha- Ha- Ha.

Slave Driver 2 is laughing wildly and screaming at the visualization of Slave Driver 1's joke, and his own involvement.

Then I told Black Tom that I was going to make him bite the snake's head off and swallow it.

They all laugh again.

Ha- Ha- Ha- Ha- Ha- Ha- Ha.

Sweat drops started falling form Black Tom and wet the whole ground all around him.

They all laugh again, braking up in laughter, slapping each other on the back. Omas and Rabbit remain silent as the Slave Drivers and overseer all laugh again loudly.

Slave Driver 1

Or was that his piss?

They all laugh again.

Ha- Ha- Ha- Ha- Ha- Ha-Ha.

Overseer Smith

Alright! Alright! Well, come on back as soon as you are able too because we can surly use you on the front lines.

Overseer Smith looks around the room as things settle down.

Now, what is this all about?

Looking to Omas and Rabbit impatiently.

Well, one of you say something, please.

Before Omas can speak.

Omas? Omas? Is this you? Omas?

Omas

Omas clears up his throat to speak.

Yes sir, Master Smith, it's Omas. And this here is my boy Rabbit.

Smiling and bring Rabbit up to his side.

Overseer Smith

Laughing and hitting his thigh.

Hot dog! It is you Omas! This farm has gotten so big and your Master Fields has gotten so many new Slaves that I don't ever see you and the old ones anymore. Have you been staying out of trouble?

Omas

Yes sir, we all be trying to stay out of trouble.

Overseer Smith

I guess you have, otherwise I would have had to see you about your troubles. So, what in the world are you doing up here today? Haven't you done got enough of me in this life time?

Omas

Avoiding eye contact with Overseer Smith.

No sir, I guess I ain't never to get enough of you Master Smith.

Overseer Smith

Now looking under eyed at Rabbit.

Omas, who is this you got with you in here?

Omas

Catching Rabbit by the arm.

Master Smith, this here is my boy Rabbit. Sir, Master Fields told me to bring my boy Rabbit up here for you to look at him, to see if he can be of some help to you in the cotton fields.

Overseer Smith

He did, did he? OooK! Bring this little Rabbit boy on over here so that I can start looking at him. So I can see if he can be of some help to me in the cotton fields. That's what your Master Fields said. Ain't it?

Omas

Yes sir.

Overseer Smith

I sure need all the help that I can get out there, but I don't need no body getting in my way

Putting on his glasses, then looking over them, getting a good look at Rabbit.

Omas, what is this little Rabbit boy doing now everyday?

Omas

Right now he totes water from the creek everyday for the washer women to wash the clothes for the big house.

Overseer Smith

Ok! Ok! That's all right.

Speaking to Little Rabbit.

How old are you boy?

Rabbit

Speaking in a low tone.

I don't know Master.

Overseer Smith

In deep thought.

Hummm. Oh yea, this is the boy that was left when Mr. Fields had to sell his mama and papa for trying to run off over and over again. It must have been something bad in their blood. Your Master Fields gave the boy to you and your woman Weeda when he was just a pup. Ain't that right Omas?

Omas

Yes sir, that's right Master Smith. You remember everything.

Overseer Smith

You are about five or six years old boy! Is that alright with you?

Rabbit

Yes sir.

Overseer Smith

Speaking triumphantly.

There Little Rabbit boy, you see, if you hang around with me, you will know about a lot of things. Some good and some bad of course. Just ask Omas about that.

Rabbit

Yes sir.

Overseer Smith

Leaning back in his big chair and putting his feet up on a low cut stump.

Ok Omas, so your Master, one Master Fields, told you to let me take a look at your boy, one Rabbit, for the purposes of seeing if I can use him in the cotton fields. Is that right?

Omas

Looking perplexed.

I think That's right Master Smith.

Overseer Smith

Looking at Little Rabbit over his glasses.

I don't know if I can use you or not boy, you might just get in my way. Let me look at your feet. Hold up your feet.

Rabbit hesitates. Overseer Smith speaks louder.

I said hold up your feet boy. Take off those rags and let me see your feet. And don't be shy because I have seen my share of black feet before.Probably more than you. Ain't that right Omas?

Rabbit

Looking at Omas for guidance,as Omas smiles at Overseer Smith's humor but received nothing but a nudge in his back. Rabbit takes off his feet coverings and stands back up straight. Overseer Smith looks closely at Rabbits feet.

Overseer Smith

Ok boy, Hold out your hands!

Rabbit holds out his hands avoiding eye contact with Overseer Smith.the way that he has always been told to do. Overseer smith looks at Rabbits feet and hands again, touching them, then wiping his hands on his handkerchief.

Now take your clothes off! All of them! Take them all off now! And don't make me have to wait on you.

Rabbit doesn't move, he just stands there trembling and with tears in his eyes.

Overseer Smith reach over and slaps Rabbit hard across the face, knocking Rabbit hard to the floor.

Rabbit boy, I told you to take your clothes off! All of them, now!

Rabbit

Yes sir, yes sir.

Omas closes his eyes, gritting his teeth, nudging Rabbit hard in the back. The other Slave drivers run back into the room from the back yard area. They run in howling and laughing loudly. Rabbit takes off all of his clothes and stands before Overseer Smith stark naked.

Slave Driver 1

You've got to see this, boy! Look at that. Oh, Oh, Oh, boy look at that! How old did you say that you are boy?

Looking at Rabbits genitals. He is ashamed and humiliated,, starts to cry.

Slave Driver 2

Ha- Ha- Ha- Ha- Ha- Ha- Ha. My God boy! Look at that! We've got to get this boy a gal, quick, to save his life! This boy is every bit of thirty five years old right now! How old did you say you are?

They all laugh and dance around again.

Ha-Ha-Ha-Ha-Ha-Ha-Ha.*Woooooo* Weeeeee, look at the tools on this boy. I need for you to tell poor me how you do it.

Overseer Smith

Speaking to the Slave Drivers.

Alright! Alright! That's enough. You all get on out of here! Get out! Get out!

The Slave Drivers all exit quickly, laughing howling their way out the door.Overseer Smith, speaking to Omas.

Omas, take your shirt off! Now don't 'you' give no trouble.Take your shirt off so that this little Rabbit boy can see what happens when any Slave on this farm don't do what I tell them to do in a hurry.

Omas takes off his shirt to expose his back to Rabbit. He turns his back to rabbit, revealing the mass of scar tissue caused by the countless whippings that he had received as a young man, for not obeying the Overseer, and for many other reasons and violations of rules that govern the lives of the enslaved.

Omas, I recommend that you impress upon this Rabbit boy that Saturdays after work is still whip day on this farm. Impress upon him also that If I am too tired on Saturday, Sundays are Just as good. Or any other day will do if need be.

Standing up over Omas and Rabbit.

You all put your clothes back on. Omas be sure to bring this little Rabbit boy to the whipping Saturday. That might help the boy to understand me better. Now! Ok! I'll send for this Rabbit boy when I get ready for him.

Meanwhile, when he gets through with his water work, have him to start helping the wood cutters hauling wood. Have him to stock up the wood sheds at the big house and then bring some wood to these quarters every day. Stack it out side in my shed. If we ever run out again we are going to send for you and this little Rabbit boy. Do you hear me Omas? Now, get this boy out of here before I nail him to the ground right now.

Omas and Rabbit are putting their clothes back on quickly while leaving the Overseers quarters.

Rabbit

Pulling onto Omas's rag shirt as they walk out the door and away from the brutal Overseer. Omas realize that they has escaped danger again, believing hopefully that he has planted a seed into Rabbits mind that will keep him alive when he has to interact with the Overseer and the Slave drivers on his own.

Papa Omas?

Omas

Gripping Rabbit by his arm, pulling him along briskly.

Don't talk right now Rabbit! Don't talk! Just walk! Fast!

Walking, they quicken their pace. After they had walked a farther distance from the Overseer's quarters, Omas looks back and sees Overseer Smith still looking at them as they walk farther away still. After a long silence while walking out of sight of the Overseers quarters Omas speaks to Rabbit again, trying to change the subject.

Rabbit, did you hear about the little boy who got drowned yesterday? He was down there swimming in that lake.

Rabbit

Stopping in his tracks.

No sir papa. Who was it that had got drowned?

Omas

I'm sorry to have to tell you but it was your friend. The one that they called Snowball.

Rabbit

Oooooh! That was my friend. I don't want to drink no more water from that lake, cause I will be drinking my friend Snowball.

Omas

You know that Weeda always boil that water before we drink it.

Rabbit

Still feeling down.

I don't care papa, I cant drink Snowball. He was my friend.

Weeda is sitting on the porch and sees Omas and Rabbit as they are coming down the trail leading to their cabin Weeda gets up and goes into the cabin. She is crying. Rabbit stops again on the trail.

Papa Omas...

Omas

Yes Rabbit.

Rabbit

Who are we?

Omas

Rabbit,,, I...

Rabbit

Papa Omas, I mean where did we all come from? And why are we different from the other kind of people like Master Smith. We are people too, ain't we? Why don't they like us? Why are we not like them?

Omas biting his lip until it bleeds, he does not answer. They walk on. Omas and Rabbit arriving at the cabin porch. They sit on the porch of the cabin for a long moment. Omas speaks to Rabbit.

Omas

Rabbit! Go around to the back at the wood pile and pick up some chips to start a fire. And get enough for in the morning.

Rabbit

Feeling dejected, goes around to the back of the cabin without going inside the house. Rabbit begin to pick up wood chips throwing them hard into the wood basket. Omas lie back on the porch and rolls over into the fetal position. Just lying there, still, facing the wall like an unborn baby. Weeda comes out of the porch wiping her face on her apron.

Weeda

What is the matter Omas? What's the matter with you honey? Why are you just laying there like that? Tell me what's the matter with you Omas?

Omas

Sitting now, facing the wall with his knees up to his chest.

While we were walking back from the Overseers quarters, that boy Rabbit asked me where we came from. He wanted to know where we all came from. And he wanted to know who we are and why we are not like white folks. And why we have to stay out here all the time like this.

Like horses and mules and chickens. And why we have to pick all this cotton, and why we have to get whipped like animals and all that. He wants to know all about these things Weeda.

Tears now in his eyes, he wipes his eyes on his rag shirt. Omas stands up and turns away from Weeda.

Weeda

Well, what did you tell the boy Omas?

Omas

Nothing! Nothing! That's what I told him. Nothing! Because I don't know nothing to tell him! I just don't know nothing! I didn't have no answers to none of his questions!

Weeda

Turning Omas around to face her, she hugs him deeply for a long moment.

It's not your fault Omas. It's not your fault. We all have been here for too long to know any of the answers to Rabbits questions.

Omas

I don't know nothing Weeda! I don't know nothing but cotton, and those mules and the whip! That's all that I know about.
Nothing else!

Weeda

I know Omas! I know! God is going to help us, that's for sure. We just have got to wait on him. He is going to help us.

After night fall, Weeda is nervously pacing the floor back and forth in the shadows and the lamp light in the small Slave cabin Rabbit is asleep on the floor pallet. When the time came Weeda walks over and blows out the lamp and touch Omas on his lips with her finger, urging him to be very quiet. Omas holds on to weeda as she pass by him on her way to the door. Weeda pull away from Omas and push his hands down. Omas

*catch her arm again and again Weeda pull harder away
from the grasp of Omas.*

Omas

Weeda! Weeda! Weeda, where are you going in the
dark honey?

Weeda

*Steps back and looks directly at Omas in the darkness
of the room.*

You stay here Omas! You just stay here and pray and
keep a look out for me!

Omas

Oh No Weeda! Please honey, don't go out there at
night, in the dark! You might get caught Weeda, honey!

Omas continues to plead with Weeda.

Weeda please don't go out there baby! If you get caught
what are we going to do? Me and Rabbit?

Weeda

I'm not going out there to get caught Omas! Just you
look out for me and pray! Just keep praying for me, and
I'll be alright! I promise you! Ok?

*Weeda hugs Omas again but pulls away from him
quickly and steps out of the back door, under the
cover of darkness. Weeda is walking as fast as she
possibly can through the dangerous clearing that is
feared by all Slaves during their days and nights
on this Smith plantation. Weeda is walking faster
than she has ever walked before even as a young
child. Weeda can barely see her hands before her
face because it is so dark. There is a moon out tonight
but at this time the moon seems to hold back it's high
shine. Weeda, struggling, trying desperately to make
it safely to the edge of the wooded area, just beyond*

the clearing. Her frail old body is so tired and her heart is beating so fast that she can no longer feel her hands, her legs nor her face. Weeda feels herself loosing consciousness. She can smell a strong smell of pine wood in her nose. She can also taste a bitter taste in her mouth that must have stopped at each and every taste bud in her mouth, traveling slowly down into her unsuspecting belly, just laying there disrupting every normal body function. This must be the taste of death, she is thinking in her mind. She may have lost consciousness for a brief time but she is so unfocused that she can not be absolutely sure. Weeda cannot walk any further even if her very life depends on it. She must rest now, or surly she will die. Weeda places her sweaty forehead into her sweaty palms pushing herself as hard as she can, throwing herself backward, hard onto the ground and falling deeper into the entrance of the wooded area.

Weeda knows that she will have time to rest now unless Master Fields, Overseer Smith, or one of the Slave Drivers or even one of the Master's spies come looking for her at her cabin tonight. She realize though that she has made it through the most dangerous part, the dangerous clearing, where any one that is outside at night can see anything or anyone moving in that area. Finally Weeda can feel the life coming back into her hands, her legs, and her face. As she finally comes to her senses she can feel the deep groves that she has scratched into the ground. She can feel the blood and dirt mingled under her frayed fingernails, and tips of her fingers feels raw. Weeda did not realize that she had crawled so far into the woods. She can hear the sounds of running water from a creek that she knows that borders the Smith plantation. Weeda is trying now to put it out of her mind the fact that she is a Slave because she is about to ask for something very big from a very big and a very mighty God that has the power to do anything that he wants to do.

Weeda is saying her own name as loud as she can to let God know that it is she that is coming, wounded and torn as she is. Weeda's name went out and up high into somewhere past this dimension into some holy place where she believes that God resides. She turns fully onto her stomach and begin to crawl deeper into the woods a few more yards and stops there at the brink of hope and despair. She leans and pushes her frail old body until she finally arrives at a kneeling position. Weeda can see the moon shining brightly through the tree canopy. She curves her tired, bleeding fingers and hands up into a praying position looking up as far as she can, as though she expects to see God himself, in all of his glory, and speaks to God. Weeda is totally exhausted.

Weeda

Whew, excuse me for a minute lord, I'm so tired from all that running, and you know that I'm kind of scary too, in all of this dark. Every time that I come out here to talk to you by myself, something good always happen to us, and I thank you for that. Like the time when I asked you to not let Master Fields catch us at our meeting that night a long time ago. We would have all been dead and gone now.

Weeda readjusting herself on her aching knees, but never taking her eyes off the highest point that she can see, looking up through the tree canopy.

Jesus we know about you and we believe you, like the others did that you wrote about in your good book. Lord Jesus you know that I'm taking a big, big chance again coming out here again to talk to you by yourself, so Lord, I need for you to please hear my cry tonight. Lord Jesus, didn't none of them tell me to come out here and talk to you for them, but lord I care about all of us folks here both the free and the bound. Cause somehow I care about them white folks too. Lord I know that you sit up high on your throne and I know that you are able to look down low on bound folks like us. Lord If we have ever did something to cause you anger at us, all I know to say is that we are all sorry. Lord we heard about how some of the people that you wrote about in your good book, sometimes brought you something. Lord Jesus I ain't got nothing to bring you cause I think the Master have his spies to count all the animals everyday. Anyway Lord Jesus I got something for you too. I caught you a little bird.

> *Weeda bring her praying hands down from their praying position searching in her apron pocket and unwraps a little bird. She tries to make the bird fly up to God, but the bird does not move nor does it try to escape. It just sits there content. Weeda gives up on trying to make the bird fly away.*

Lord, we don't even know where we are in this land, but we know for sure Lord Jesus, that all freedom in the whole world belongs to you. So, So I need for you to help me to get some of these boys over to the free side. And Lord I need for you to help me to trick these old Slave Catchers, so they won't be able to catch and spoil these boys no more. And Lord I need for you to show us the way how to get there to the free side. Lord we need for you to help us if you please. Lord the White folks is so mean to us here that they treat the cows and the mules and chickens and such as that, better than they treat us. And one more thing Lord Jesus. Lord bless my man Omas. He is a good man and he always try to do the right things by people. And Lord bless my boy Rabbit that you gave us. Help him to grow up strong and sturdy. And Lord bless all the others and help us to bear all the burdens that is on all of us. And oh yes, Lord one more thing. Me and Omas has got this misery in our backs and our heads, and it hurts so bad sometimes. I guess it's from all of those work years. Sometimes the misery is in our chest and our legs, all of us old ones. So, please come to see about us and protect us with all your might like the ones you wrote about in your good book. Thank you Lord Jesus, good by.

Without warning Weeda feels a strong jerk on her neck from behind her. The strong hand moves from her neck to her mouth. She feels a sharp pointed blade pushing hard against her stomach. She is being wrestled and pulled like an animal until she finally succumbs to this persons strength and the possibility of being choked to death or even to be cut open like an animal right here in these woods. She thought about Omas and Rabbit and also about the reason that she had came into these woods tonight. She continues to look up as high as she can as she cease to resists this person, and she sees that the tree canopy is unchanged. The only change is that the moon is now visible. The moon is looking so calm and majestic and seems to be an unwitting witness to all that is happening to her, but it is known that moons don't tell. The power and strength of this person behind her and the uncertainty of the outcome of all of this fight overwhelms Weeda's thoughts as the blade pushes harder and harder against her stomach. Weeda has been caught completely off guard and she knows it. Weeda can now smell a strong pungent stench filling her mouth her nose and lungs like of which she has never smelled before, except maybe when she had found the carcass of a wild animal when she was a little girl.

The good warm feeling that Weeda was feeling moments before when she was communicating with God, is now gone, replaced with the feeling of the need to fight for her life or even to a greater extent, the need to just survive what ever is taking place behind her in the dark of night on this cold damp ground. The bad taste in her mouth that she had experienced before is now back again, forcing it's way past her old worn taste buds again dripping slowly into her stomach causing her to feel weak and nauseous again.

Freedom Woman

Be quiet old woman! Be quiet! Stop moving! Don't say anything! Don't even breathe or I will gut you right here like a pig! Do you understand me? Just listen for now, I will tell you when to talk!

Weeda stopped breathing freely. She inhaled and exhaled only when it was absolutely necessary. She can hear herself swallow between her measured breaths.

I'm not going to wait on you like I did before. Do you understand me? You made me have to wait twice before!

Weeda

Yes, but I....

Weeda, trying to explain herself.

Freedom Woman

Stop talking! Don't say nothing!! Just listen to me! I've got a bone to pick with you!

Pulling Weeda's head back and pushing her knife harder to Weeda's Stomach.

On the third moon high! On the third moon high! I'm not going to wait on you. Some died because of you the last time, so don't make me have to sit here and wait. And don't send me nobody, that can't run.

Don't- make- me- have- to- wait- on you! Do you understand me?

Weeda

Yes...Yes... I understand you. I won't be late.

The strong hand releases Weeda's throat and the knife is removed from her stomach. Weeda, speaking slightly above a whisper.

Aaah… That voice! I know that voice when we was girls here! You was the only girl that Master Fields ever whipped himself. He sold you because you wasn't scared of him. I remember you! You told Master Fields to his face that you were going to get him. You're getting him now ain't you?

Weeda turns around to see the girl she knew who is now an old woman also. No one is there! Weeda can hear the Freedom Woman crawling away in the dark. She does not try to follow her or to see her crawling away. Weeda is back in her right mind again, she feels as though she has been in the very presence of royalty tonight. She feels also as though she is returning from such a powerful place that if she had a choice, she would have stayed. Weeda begins her journey back, walking fast as she can through the dangerous clearing. Thinking that she has heard something, she falls to the ground and remain motionless for a time. She then continue to walk fast as she can through and around the edge of this dangerous clearing. Again weeda is out of breath, hardly able to stand on her feet when she reach the back door of the Slave cabin. She pushes the door open, falling past Omas to the floor of the Slave Cabin. Omas who is standing in the half opened back door, falls to the floor with Weeda. She grabbs Omas as she is falling, pulling him hard down with her. She is desperately trying to catch her breath gripping Omas with all of the strength left in her old frail body. They both just lie there on the floor in each others arms. Omas never questions Weeda as to where she has been. They just lay there.

Weeda

Between deep breaths.

Omas! Omas! Were going to have a meeting tomorrow night. I need for you to let everyone know. The ones that came the last time when we had a meeting. Only those that we know that we can trust. Ok? Tell them all to come after dark, to this cabin, just like before.

Omas does not answer, just smiles broadly in the dark. Shaking his head, smiling and admiring the woman that he loves more than he loves even himself. They both fall asleep on the floor.

END OF SCENE TWO

Act: 1

Scene: 3

Scene three takes place inside the Slave cabin of Omas and Weeda. There are no windows. About ten trusted Slaves and a few children are present in the cabin. The small Slave cabin is almost filled to it's capacity. Some Slaves are sitting on the floor, some are also standing around the wall. A rolled up bed pallet is in one corner and a lamp is on a tree stump in the center of the room. There is also a crude looking wood stove that is in the center of the semi-circle of Slaves. The children are ushered to where the bed pallet is rolled up in the corner. There are low murmurs in the Slave cabin as the Slaves sit impatiently waiting. Waiting for the last few Slaves to arrive so that the meeting can begin. They wait also to find out just what is on Weeda's mind this time. The lamp is turned down lower, and the lighting is so that the faces of the Slaves that are present, are shadowed. The close proximity of the Slaves and the lack of air circulation in this small room causes them all to sweat heavily. The last of the expected Slaves are now arriving, taking their places, until they soon blend in among all the other black bodies and faces. Two watchful and trusted Slaves are posted at points outside the Slave cabin to watch and pray that no one stumble up on them in their meeting in the dark. If so, all will be warned.

Young Child

Standing up from her mothers grasp.

What are we going to do tonight, aunt Weeda?

Weeda ignores the child's question.

Are we going to learn to read tonight, aunt Weeda.

John H.Hall

Weeda

Be quiet child!

Responding to the child, standing up, moving in front of the sweating group of black faces, taking charge of the meeting.

No child! We ain't here to learn no reading. I want you children to get up and move on over there to that pallet, sit down and be quiet.

Weeda motions for Rabbit to come to her. She grabs him by his arm, turning him around.

You all know my boy Rabbit, don't you? You all know that my boy Rabbit don't lie to me for nothing, don't you?

Turning Rabbit all around so that all the shadowed faces can see him.

Tell them what you heard at the creek today Rabbit. Go on and tell them.

Rabbit

Nervously, looking at Weeda.

Aaaa...

Weeda

Don't look at me, look at them!

Rabbit

Facing the black, shadowed faces, clearing up his throat.

Aaammm, when I was at the creek today bringing water for the washer women, I heard the white men talking. They was talking about that Freedom Woman. They said that she was helping more Slaves to escape to freedom. They said that they had got word that the

Freedom Woman was heading this way, to these parts. I couldn't hear too much after that because they stopped talking to drink some of my water. Then I had to leave with my bucket of water and the water was heavy.

Rabbit beams excitedly then sit back down on the floor with the other children.

Weeda

Pointing her finger towards the outside.

You all head that! You heard it for your self. That Freedom Woman is here in these parts again. I said, that Freedom Woman is here again! What Rabbit is telling you has got to be true because that old Master Fields came asking questions again. And this time he brought some young turtle with him and they tried to rough me and Omas up. He can beat us and kick us. He can do anything that he want to do to us but, we ain't talking! We just want to be free!

Smiling to herself.

Master Fields said to our faces that the Freedom Woman is helping more Slaves from other farms to escape. So she 'is' in these parts. Right now! She is here now! While these reb soldiers are talking about holding us back, the blue coats are turning their heads and letting us go. I ain't never seen that Master Fields so worked up, ever. He is deadly scared! could see it in his eyes! I could hear it in his talk! I'm telling you that she is here!!

Slave Woman 1

Standing, voice trembling.

Now ms. Weeda, you have already sent off four boys, all motherless and fatherless children. All in the last few years, and they are all dead! Ms. Weeda, you know that those dirty Slave Catchers all just spoil these boys dead bodies. It's hardly anything left for us to bury. And there was that one boy that they found dead by the swamps for trying to run off on his own.

Looking around at the shadowed faces.

These young boys ain't no match for these Slave Catchers Ms. Weeda. And the Snakes and the other animals just about ate them all up...

Weeda

Cutting the Slave Woman off before she finishes. Weeda speaks very calmly at first.

Child, you're just looking at what's happening today. You've got to look at tomorrow, and the next day, and the next day and on and on. We can't just keep staying here with no hope at all. We have got to get some of these children out to the free side right now!!

Slave Woman 2

Standing to her feet, speaking in anger.

Woman ain't you got enough of this killing up these boys? Right now, when you look around, it ain't hardly no boys left on this farm place now, just because of nobody but you Weeda. No body but you Weeda! It's you that's killing all of these boys! Just killing up our children. You! You!

Crying, looking around at the other sweating black faces.

We're bound to be here Weeda. Where can we go to keep you from killing these boys?

The shadowed figures stir uneasily in the room, some agreeing with the Slave Woman 2.

Weeda

Moving around confronting every shadowed face.

These young boys have got strong arms, I tell you! These young boys have got strong legs. And they have got strong hearts. Some of these boys can run all day long.

Striking her palm with her fist.

These boys are strong because they are warriors, and not Slaves! They know when to hide and they know when to fight. These boys don't want to be no Slave! They want to be free boys! They will fight if they have to, because they are not Slaves, so we have got to get some of them to the free side!

Slave Woman 1

Then why are they all dead Weeda? Since they are all such great warriors, why are they all dead? Huh?

Weeda

Walking back and forth in front of the shadowed faces.
The group of Slaves continue to murmur.

Be quiet! Listen! Listen! I want you to hear me well!! Some of us have lived out our whole lives right here on this farm grounds, and we still ain't got no hope. None of us in this room don't even know what's on the other side of that clearing.

Pointing outside.

Don't look at me like I'm a fool. We ought to be ashamed of our selves. We ought to be trying to run ourselves, but most of us are too old to run now. Some of you just came here to this farm. You need to run! Do you hear me? So you can come back under ground to help more of us to run. Some of these strong young boys need to run to freedom like that Under Ground Woman. Some have got to try!

Screaming at the faces.

Some have got to die! Some have got to die! Do you hear me?? Some have got to die!

Weeda continues. Now pacing in front of the shadowed, black, sweating faces.

Now, who is willing to send their boy to freedom? Don't you see? I've got to ask you this because this is for all of us.

Looking around, her eyes beginning to fill up with tears, still no one speaks.

I said, who is willing to send their boy to freedom? We have got to sacrifice some of our own, because this not right to us, nor is it right to those who come after we are gone. We have 'got' to get some of these boys out to the free side. We need some more hope, don't you understand any of this?

Confronting every face again.

Cotton! Cotton! That's all that we understand. And you all sing all day just like you like it out there in that hot sun chopping and pulling cotton all day long. Don't you want to be free? Me and Omas picked that white devil until we was cotton blind. Everything that we see look like white dots to us. Most of you all are young now but you'll see what I mean, you just keep on getting up in the mornings. Then you'll be crying like me.

Continuing to pace back and forth in front of the Black, shadowed faces, challenging each one of them.

Do you want your girl child to be brought up to be breeder women, breeding like animals until they are barren? Do you want your boy child to be raised in this old Slavery camp, like those critters out there?

The crowd of black sweating Slaves murmurs.

Do you want your children put out to pasture, like old Liza there and old Margi, and like me and Omas. Ten babies and I ain't got none of them with me. I wouldn't know any of them from Adam.

The Black faces looks caring but no one speaks. Weeda continues to search their every expression. Now speaking calmly, catching her breath.

Ok! That Freedom Woman is gonna come through hear real soon. They say that she is already in these parts. We don't have no time to loose. She is probably out there cold and wet at night, laying low.

Weeda pauses, then after a long silence she speaks.

I'm going to send my boy Rabbit!!

Bracing for the outrage. The murmurs are dangerously loud as the Slaves present are truly outraged.

Shhhhheeeeeeee!!

Weeda puts her finger up to her lips to silence the crowd, but their outrage continues.

That's right! Yes, you heard me right! I'm going to send my boy Rabbit to freedom!!

Rabbit stands up and moving closer to Weeda and beaming broadly.

Slave Woman 3

You're a fool, Weeda! We are all just Slaves here, and we are just going to be Slaves until Jesus comes to save us. Just tell me, why are you going to kill your own child Weeda? Just tell me that! What will happen if Little Rabbit gets there too late, or even too early? Those old Slave Catchers will be there waiting on him. Waiting to kill and spoil what's left of him!

Slave Woman 1

Weeda, If you're going to send Little Rabbit to die out there, then why are you still looking for more boys to send? I believe that you're foolish enough to send a new born baby out there to meet that Freedom Woman if you could.

Still other voices pound Weeda's plans. Omas is seated on the floor by the door, occasionally going outside to check on the watcher men.

Anyway, how is Little Rabbit going to know which way to go once he get past that clearing? That's why they are dying, they get lost out there, Weeda. Those Slave Catchers knows every inch of this land just like it's the back of their hands.

Weeda

Weeda's ready response seems to aid her position.

I know that the star that's so bright in the sky every night is the North Star, and it will take you there. It's always facing the north the same way no matter which way that you turn. You just follow it until you get to the north. I guess you will be right under the North Star when you get there. I ain't never forgot that, and I never will.

Again challenging the faces.

You just think about that Freedom Woman. She probably went to Freedom just like Little Rabbit is going to go.

A look of pride creases Little Rabbit's face again.

And not only that, they have got a reward on her head. Do You know why?

Because she must be kicking up some sand.

In anger, Weeda hit down on the hot stove and jerks her hand away quickly. Some of the Slave Women try to look a Weeda's burn but she pull away from them and sits down on a stump by the stove. The other Slave Women all sit back down.

Is there anyone here who is willing to start the end to this Slavery now, tonight? Is there anyone here who is willing to send their boy to Freedom with my boy, Little Rabbit?

Weeda looks around again but no one answers. She shakes her head slowly, then takes off her old worn shoe and violently throws it against the wall, knocking over the kettle on the stove, splashing root tea on the floor and against the wall. With this act, a little girl stands up and tries to speak but her mother grabs the child's mouth and arm, pulling her back down hard. Weeda look away to avoid the child's eyes, as the child's eyes are burning with interest and anticipation.

That Freedom Woman will be close to these parts in a few days for sure. A few days!! A few days!!

Getting up ending the meeting in a prayer.

Lord I thank you for letting us meet here safe. I pray lord that you let us all return back to our cabin safe. Pleas bless everyone of us and don't let the Master or his spies know about this meeting. Thank you Jesus!

While the group slips out quietly, Weeda speaks.

I want to thank you all for coming to hear what had to say. Please leave one at a time and please be careful and quiet. Remember, that Freedom Woman is just like you and me! She ain't going to wait for us all year long to come out and show ourselves, and prove that we want to be free people too. I'm going to send my boy Rabbit! I've got to send him!

Low scream, then muffled screams.

Can't you understand that some got to die! Some got to die!

But my boy Rabbit is going to live!

END OF SCENE 3

Act: 1

Scene: 4

As scene four opens, we find Weeda coming out of the back door of the Slave Cabin into the back yard area to feed the chickens. She has the chicken feed in her apron pocket, slowly walking around among the chickens, dropping small amounts of feed onto the ground. The chickens scurry about, pecking up every piece of feed as soon as it hits the ground. The chickens the wait, anticipating the next dropped bit of feed. Weeda is remembering all the things that has happened in the last few days. There continues to be a feeling of dissatisfaction in her demeanor. Weeda is brought back to the present by the voice of a young girl. The young girls hands are tugging at her apron.

Tweety Bird

Good morning, Aunt Weeda.

Weeda

Well, good morning to you my little Tweety Bird.How are you this morning?

Tweety Bird

I'm doing fine.

Weeda

What in the world are you doing up so early in the morning, little girl?

Tweety Bird

Looking guilty

I slipped away from my keeper.

Weeda

Looking sternly at Tweety.

Now, you know better than that! I ought to put my switch on you! What if you get caught away from where you're suppose to be?

Tweety Bird

I don't care because my keeper don't care. Just as long as I'm with you, because everybody likes you.

Holding out her hands.

Can I help you feed the chickens? Can I help you please?I just love chickens.

Weeda

Yes,I know you do. You just love to eat them up when they are fried all good and brown, and there is some of those good old biscuits on the table, and some sweet syrup.

They both laugh and laugh.

Ha- Ha- Ha- Ha- Ha- Ha- Ha- Ha- Ha- Ha-Ha-Ha.

Tweety Bird

Yumm - Yumm - Yumm.

They both laugh again.Weeda puts Tweety's hand in her apron pocket and let her get a big handful of chicken feed. Tweety tosses one grain of feed out at a time as they move along slowly through the back yard area. Weeda and tweety sit down on and old bench against the back wall of the Slave Cabin. Tweety continues to playfully pluck down the morsels of feed to the chickens, one at a time. Weeda notices that Tweety is looking very sad.

Weeda

Child, what is on your little mind this morning?You want to talk to Aunt Weeda, don't you?

Tweety Bird

Yes mamm.

Getting close to weeda, jumping excitedly and looking up at her.

Tell me about freedom land please Aunt Weeda. Where is this freedom land at Aunt Weeda? Have you ever been there? Can any one go to freedom? What about me Aunt Weeda? Can I go? Can I go to freedom.

Weeda

Weeda is frozen in her action and her speech, looking puzzled.

Slow down child! You slow down right there! You have asked me every question that you never ought to be asking me. Where did you get all of that kind of talk from? Now you listen to me good!

Grabs Tweety by both of her shoulders.

Now you listen to me good girl! I don't want to hear you say another word about freedom, ever again. Do you hear me?? I said, do you hear me??

Tweety does not answer.

I want you to forget everything that you know about freedom land. Do you hear me?

Again Tweety does not answer.

If the Master ever hear you say that word to me he will kill me! Do you want Aunt Weeda to get killed?

Tweety Bird

Looking sad and defiant at the same time.

No mamm!

Weeda

Letting Tweety's arms go, the a long silence.

So many questions. No baby girl, Aunt Weeda ain't never been to freedom land, but I've been trying to get there since I was a little gal like you.

Weeda is shaking her head. She begin to touch Tweety's hair trying desperately to change this hard subject.

My, my, my, you have got some pretty, pretty hair. Some strong course hair like mine used to be, and you're a pretty gal.

Tweety continues to ask painful questions.

Aunt Weeda, my keeper says that you know a lot about freedom. She said that you're going to send some more children to freedom again, but they're going to die.

Tweety looking sad.

Are they going to die, Aunt Weeda? Are they going to die?

Weeda

Looking and feeling proud.

No baby girl, not this time! They're not going to die this time! No they are 'not' going to die.

Tweety Bird

Leaping to her feet screaming.

You mean that they're not going to die??

Tweety grabs the hem of Weeda's apron, throwing the entire handful of chicken feed to the chickens at one time. The chickens leap on the abundance of chicken feed.

Ohhhh, Ohhhh, Ohhhh, Aunt Weeda, Aunt Weeda. Ohhhh, Ohhhh, Ohhhh, Aunt Weeda, Aunt Weeda.

Please, please, let me go. Can I go to freedom? Please, please will you send me to freedom? They're not going to die!! Can I go?? Can I go, Aunt Weeda? I can read a little bit Aunt Weeda!! Little sue has been showing me how to read a little bit! Can I go?? Can I go to freedom? Can I go?

Weeda

Looking way off with tears in her eyes, pushing Tweety Bird away from her, pushing her hard to the ground.

No child!! No! You're a girl child! Don't you understand! You're a girl child! It's got to be a boy child!

Tweety

Whining

Aaooooww, why can't I go to freedom just because I'm a girl? Why? Why? Why can't I be the one to go?? I can run almost as fast as Rabbit. And I can run faster than Bubba because one time when we

Weeda

Interrupting and speaking hard to Tweety Bird.

No! I said no, and I mean it! No! And that's all there is to it. Do you hear me. And that's that. Don't say another word about it!! Now you go on back to your keeper! Right now, Git!! Hitting Tweety Bird hard on her behind. Go on, Git!!

Tweety Bird

Running out a few yards from Weeda with her head down. Tears building up in her eyes. She stands there for

a long second. She then jerks her head up with a gleam in her eyes like of which Weeda has never witnessed in a child ever before. Weeda bites her lip hard as she can to keep from crying out loud and screaming at Tweety Bird at the very top of her lungs, but she manages to supress it all. Tweety is unable to control her emotions.
She screams out loud to Weeda.

I don't care, I want to go to freedom!!   I don't care, I want to go to freedom!!

END OF SCENE 4

Act: 1

Scene: 5

Scene five opens on the front porch of the same Slave Cabin in which the play begin. The time is one day after scene four. There are two old Slave Women shelling peas sitting on the edge of the porch. Weeda is sitting on the porch rocking in her rocking chair, she is shelling peas also. there is something in the air. Omas comes around the cabin.

Weeda

Shelling peas like there is no tomorrow. The Slave Women both stop shelling their peas and are just staring at Weeda.

Why are both of you cows staring at me like that? You had better put your eyes on these peas and stop gawking at me, that is if you intend to eat some of them.

Omas

Laughing out loud.

Ha- Ha- Ha- Ha. You all ain't got to eat none of them, I'll eat all of you alls part.

Slave Woman 1

Stamping her feet hard.

Stop it Weeda! Stop it! You just stop it right now! You can't fool no body. We got a bad feeling about you. Like you are about to do something that's really, really bad! And Weeda you ain't never been that interested in shelling no peas.

Slave Woman 2

That's right! That's right! We know you too well Weeda! You ain't got none of us fooled. You ain't never worked that fast since I ever known you. And that's been a mighty long time.

Weeda didn't realize that she has been tearing the peas out of their pods, and that the peas and hulls are all over the porch.

Weeda

Looking up from her work, giving in to the two Slave Women.

Ok! Ok! Ok! You asked me, and you wont leave me alone about it. I'm going to send my boy Rabbit to freedom...Tonight!! Just when the Master and the Slave Catchers are sitting down eating their supper. Just when they have already put up the horses and the dogs. Just when their mind is not on it...I'm going to send him! I'm going to do it...Tonight!!

Weeda, waiting for one of them to say something hard to her, but no one says anything. Omas does not look surprised. The Slave Women just look at each other in amazement, but no one speaks.

Weeda

Now! Now! That's what you wanted to hear from me. Now you've heard it. I'm going to send my boy Rabbit alone... Tonight!!

Slave Woman 1

Spellbound

I guess you and Omas has already planned this? Weeda, child please! Please listen to me this time! Don't do this Weeda! Please! This is your own child. God gave him to you and Omas. Don't you realize that? Those old Slave Catchers will be out here as soon as they hear those dog and horses acting up. The dogs and the horses will tell it on you. They will know Weeda! They will come from all around to help find him. They will kill Little Rabbit!

Weeda

Weeda is now tearing the peas out of their pods again.

Now is the right time. The time is right. Rabbit can meet that Freedom Woman, cause most of the Slave Catchers are away from here anyway, trying to fight a war and such as that. I tell you that the time is right cause that Freedom Woman is here in these parts again, right now.We can't let this good chance get by us. The time is right for us. Those Blue Coats are turning their heads to all that we do.

Slave Woman 1

Weeda, a little boy just can't out smart those Slave Catchers, because that's all that they do is track and catch run away Slaves. Woman, these are Slave Catchers!! They are not normal kind of people. That's all that they do Weeda!!

Weeda continue to tear the peas out of their pods. She is not listening. She will not listen. She will not let Rabbit listen, and she knows that Omas will not listen. Weeda must make it work this time because this could be her last chance to get one of these children out to meet this Freedom Woman.

END OF SCENE 5

Act: 1

Scene: 6

Scene six opens at dust dark, on the late evening of scene five. Weeda has Rabbit standing in a corner by the back door of the Slave Cabin. We find Weeda tying on Rabbit's shoes tightly. She is doing her best to function at this critical time. She is remembering that so much has happened in so little time.

Weeda

Speaking to Rabbit.

Rabbit, did you get a good nap?

Rabbit

No mam, I couldn't sleep too much.

Looking at his shoes and flexing his feet in his new shoes.

Mama Weeda, these are my good shoes.

Weeda

I know Rabbit. These are the shoes that Mama want you to ware. Ok?

Weeda continues to dress Rabbit, wrapping his arms and legs with rags that are soaked in some type of solution.

The dogs and the horses can't smell you with this stuff on you. Ok?

Rabbit

Trying to smell himself, smiling. Omas enter the room from the outside. Darkness can be seen outside when the door is opened. Omas has two draw string bags with enough food that can last Rabbit for a few days. Omas gives Weeda one of the bags, without looking at her or Rabbit. Omas is looking very sad. Rabbit is eager to be on his way to freedom, but Weeda is holding on to him for dear life. A lump forms in Weeda's throat causing her to touch her throat to help herself to swallow. She didn't need to prime Rabbit or give him a pep talk, because he is ready to go to his freedom. Weeda is crying huge tears now. Rabbit's anticipation is over the top of his little being. He begin to prance in place impatiently like a young pony that is fighting to free himself from his misunderstood captivity. Weeda tugs at Rabbit's arm again, touching his head and touching him all over to make sure that everything is in place.

Omas

Here, this is something else, this will help to keep you safe.

Omas places something in Rabbits pocket. He is rubbing an oil solution on his head and face again.

Weeda

Now Rabbit, you stay by the swamps, Do you hear me ? Don't- walk- by- the- main- road, or the main trail. Ok? If you see or even hear some horses or dogs, I want you to just stop and be just as still as you can. Ok? This is some more stuff, so they wont be able to smell you or see you.

Weeda is more nervous than Rabbit.

Don't move around too much when it's day time. Ok? And here, take this.

Handing Rabbit a good luck charm.

The old water man sent this to you to make your journey safe. Now, if one of those Slave Catchers catch up to you and mean to do you harm, I want you to put this lucky charm in your mouth boy and I want you to bite down hard on it. Bite down hard on it and I want you to fight to kill any body that's close to you that mean to do you harm. Do you hear me Rabbit? That probably wont happen but just to be sure, Run if you can, but if you can't get away, I want you to fight for your life if you have to. But don't be looking for no fight. Ok?

Rabbit

Yes mam, I will fight them if I have to, and I'm gong to win the fight! Weeda pulls Rabbit towards the door making last minute adjustments on his clothes and wraps. Rabbit is relieved that all this preparation is over, thinking that finally he will be going to freedom with the other free people.

Weeda

Mama and papa can't go to freedom with you right now Rabbit, You are a man now. I want you to act like a big man. Don't play around along the way. I want you to stay focused and always keep a look out for anything that ain't right.

Looking deep into Rabbit's eyes.

You don't have to look for that Freedom Woman. Ok? You just keep running the way that I show you and she will find you and I want you to do everything that she tell you to do.

Weeda, taking Rabbit out the back door and into the dark of night that seems to be showing off every star in the vast heavens.

Now listen to me good! Listen to me carefully. I want you to forget everything that you have ever heard about freedom, and just do what I tell you to do. Ok? Do you see that bright star right there?

Pointing to the north star.

Rabbit

Yes mam, I see that really bright star right there.

Pointing

Weeda

That's the north star. That's where you are going, to the north.

That's the way to where freedom land is. Remember, if you only move around at night, that bright, north star will always be there to guide you. All that you've got to do is look up and look for that brightest star every night. Do you understand what I'm saying?

Rabbit

Prancing in place like a young dear.

Yes mam! Yes mam! Yes mam!
Can I go now?

Weeda

Ok! Ok! You be sure that every time that you look around, that you see that bright shining star shining on your back, and you'll be heading the right way. Ok? You be sure that every time that you look around, that you see that bright star shining over your shoulder.

Weeda holds on to Rabbit's hand for as long as she can. Rabbit's hand slowly slides out of Weeda's hand ans she tries to hold on To it but it's too late Rabbit is gone. Rabbit is off like a young buck, running like a young pony, or even like a young Jack Rabbit, moving through the night. Rabbit looks over his shoulder occasionally, placing the brightest star in the night skies, right in the center of his back just like his mother has told him to do. Weeda and Omas watch Rabbit until he is swallowed up by the night.

They stand there arm in arm and in complete silence for what seems like hours, days, weeks, months and even years, until they can hear the slave population moving around preparing to push out to work from their Slave quarters. The moon is still high but the moon seem to be stalling in it's high shine, but nothing can prevent the coming of the first sign of daylight.

Weeda and Omas slowly comes back to their present reality, and they realize the impact of what they have just done and they are in fear of their lives. Weeda starts to move around quickly causing Omas to notice that something else is wrong. Weeda is speaking slightly incoherent to Omas, but he does hear her clear enough. Weeda speaks to Omas!

Omas, go and tell the Overseer Smith that Rabbit is gone. Tell him that Rabbit was gone when we woke up a while ago.

Omas, then go to the big house and tell all the house workers too. Tell them all that Rabbit is gone, and be sure to tell them all which way that you think that Rabbit might have ran. And Omas, cause as much commotion as you can without letting on. And Omas, be sure that Master Fields hear about it too if he is at the house. After that, You don't know nothing else. Alright?

Omas takes off, moving as fast as his frail body will move. It is still dark and the moon is still up high somewhat as Weeda watch Omas disappear, moving toward the Overseers quarters and the main house. As soon as Omas is out of sight of Weeda, She runs into the house quickly, and runs out again as fast as she can. Weeda jumps off the porch fast. She is carrying a draw string bag. She enters the wooded area on the rear side of the clearing, murmuring incoherently to herself. Weeea continues:

Where are you at gal? Show yourself right now! Come to me gal!! Come on out right now! Show yourself!

A small shadowy figure moves toward Weeda. It is little Tweety Bird.

Ok! So you say that you can run?? God knows that you had better be able to run! Are you ready to run for your life, and run for my life too?

Tweety Bird

Yes mam, I'm ready to run right now.

Prancing in place.

Weeda

Just hold on for a minute.

Weeda, handing Tweety Bird the draw string bag and turning her around to face the wooded area across the dangerous crossing while still talking to her.

Didn't you tell me that you wanted to go to freedom?

Tweety Bird

Yes mam, I'm ready to run right now.

Weeda

There it is! There it is right there!

Weeda, pointing to the dark clearing directly ahead of them.

Do you remember everything that I told you?

Tweety Bird

Yes mam I remember everything that you told me to do. And you told me to come back for you all after I get my freedom.

Weeda

That Freedom woman is waiting for you over by those trees. That's your freedom gal! Can you see her over there??

Tweety

Looking around at the tree line straight ahead of them. She can see a shadowy figure at the tree line. Tweety feels something jump inside of her that lifts her young body completely up off the ground, but lands her safely again to the damp ground.

I see her, I see her, right there! I see her Aun't Weeda! Can I go now?? Can I go to freedom now?

Weeda

It's time to run little girl! I mean you better run! Run and don't look back.I want you to run until you can't run no more. And don't look back for nothing! Go on now, git! Git on gal, git! I don't care what happens, what ever you do don't come back here for nothing. Just keep running til you get your freedom. Just do everything that the Freedom Woman tell you to do.Now go! Git!

Weeda pushes Tweety Bird hard in the back and hit her hard on her behind. Tweety Bird takes off running. She can feel the wind on her face and body like she never has before. She can feel her body drifting, floating and feeling free for the first time in her young life. She looks back at Weeda and see Weeda and Omas standing there. She waves at them but never stops running. Weeda can still hear Tweety Bird when she meet The Freedom Woman there.

Tweety Bird

Jumping up and down when she arrive at the Freedom Woman's station.

I'm not tired!! I'm not tired! I can still run some more!!

END OF SCENE SIX

Act: 1

Scene: 7

Scene seven takes place in the back yard area of Weeda's and Omas's Slave Cabin. We find Weeda taking her time hanging up a few old clothes that she has washed out, and occasionally dropping a few morsels of chicken feed to the chicken who faithfully follow her around the yard. She patiently hums an old hymn that she remembers the old folk used to sing when she was a little girl herself.

The fact that this is a perfect day really supprises Weeda. The right amount of sun was shining through the correctly spaced clouds in the sky.The right amount of wind is blowing from the right directions at the right times. She is remembers just how really good that God is and has been to her and her family such as it is. She remembers to be careful to not complain about how she is living today, because the day is so pretty. Just a picture perfect day that only God can make.

This scene takes place also only ten or twelve hours after the daybreak that had broken into so many pieces for Weeda and Omas. Weeda knows though that the circumstances of the morning will not let this beautiful day last for too much longer. She does feel a little tense in her spirit. The entire Slave population has joined the Slave Catchers in their search for Rabbit, searching on the plantation grounds, on the Overseer's orders. Weeda, Omas, and a few other Slaves are not allowed to search for Rabbit because something about they must first be cleared of any suspicion of playing any part. in the escape.

Without warning, the once peaceful morning is shattered. Weeda screams loudly, and tries to run when she see three Slave Women converging on her with sticks and chains. *The angry Slave Women, blitzing Weeda, hitting her hard, causing her to move away from them, falling to the ground. Omas comes from nowhere, quickly stepping between the Women and Weeda. Omas stops them sharply.*

Omas

Stop! Stop that! What's wrong with you all. Leave Weeda alone! What has gotten into you women? The devil must be in you all!

Omas standing firmly between the Slave Women and Weeda.

Slave Woman

Where is my child, you cow?? Where is my Tweety Bird?? Tell me where she is… right now! Where is my gal?? I'm not fooling around with you. You big cow!

Omas struggles to keep the Slave Women away from Weeda.

Get out of our way Omas! Cause I just might hit you too! I mean it! Where is she?? Tell me where she is or I'll hit you again! My child must have been gone all night and you're there looking like you ain't done nothing. I know you Weeda! I know you Weeda! I know that you had something to do with it. Where is she, you cow??

Weeda

Laying on the ground, holding her head, with Omas standing over preventing the Slave Women from hitting her again.

Why did You all have to hit me on my head? You all know that I am sick!

Looking towards heaven.

Lord God, Jesus! Please don't let them hit me anymore. I don't even know what you all are talking about.

Slave Woman

Drawing back the stick again.

We're going beat your brains out if you don't tell me where my gal Tweety bird is! I mean for you to know that I'm not fooling around with you! Tell me where she is??

The Slave Women, Weeda and Omas are all startled at the sounds of horses coming into their hearing and seeing range. Lt. Downs is riding by them on his horse, in his dusty Confederate Uniform. He is looking down long and hard at Omas as he rides by them. He is riding with his bridle free hand resting firmly on his confederate revolver, pushing the handle away from his body. Lt. Downs does not say anything as he rides by, but his horse is creating a giant dust cloud that validates him again, that respectfully follow him again in all of his believed glory and in all of his believed supremacy. In that same instant there is heard loud laughter, loud screams and yells. The Slaves all turn around in hopes of seeing Tweety Bird standing there. To their disappointment they see that is the Slave Catchers are laughing and howling the way that they always do when they have caught a run away Slave. Nothing else could possibly make them this happy. Their baritone voices bellows at the top of their lung capacity. The Slave Catchers continue their laughing and howling, staggering and falling to the ground and getting back up again only to fall intentionally again. They are drinking whisky out of a whisky jug and passing the jug around to each other.

Slave Catcher 1 & 2

...and I mean that he was running just like a wild Jack Rabbit!

More laughter and hoots.

Ha- Ha- Ha- Ha- Ha- Ha- Ha- Ha... Whhhoooopp.... Ha- Ha- Ha- Ha. He- He- He- He- He- He- He- He... OOOoooWowwwwwww.

I mean, I mean he was running dead south,,, dead south!! The wrong way!! Now he is a dead Rabbit!! Yes, a very dead Rabbit! Yeaaaa, Yeaaaa,

A very dead Jack Rabbit! Ha- Ha- Ha- Ha- Ha- Ha- Ha- Ha- Ha- Ha- Ha. Yeaa, Yea, Whoooop!!

Overseer Smith

Overseer smith enters carrying the lifeless body of Rabbit on his shoulder. Rabbit is covered with his blood, and is very disfigured. The Slave catchers continue to laugh, stagger around, passing the whisky jug among each other, then dancing the jig with Rabbit's lifeless body on their shoulder, passing him around to each other.

He could have lost us for a while, but he did us a good favor. He left us a clear trail. Ha- Ha- Ha- Ha- Ha- Ha- Ha- Ha.

Weeda, Omas, and the three Slave Women all turn and look at each other in a strange but now peaceful way, despite the condition of Rabbit.Overseer smith turns Rabbits body over on the rich black soil standing over him in triumph.

The good luck charm that had been given to Rabbit can still be seen between Rabbits teeth. Rabbit died fighting, and with a look of determination on his face. The Slaves followed the Slave Catchers with their eyes and bodies, turning, watching them as they stagger drunkenly away. Weeda and Omas gently spread a blanket over Rabbit's body then in a sudden burst of screams and laughter, they begin to dance and jump for joy. The Slave Women throw their sticks high into the air as they continue to dance and shout for joy.

Jesus! Jesus! Jesus! Thank you Jesus! Thank you sweet Jesus! OOOh, Jesus! OOOh, we love you sweet Jesus. Thank you Jesus!

The Slave Women and Omas form a tight circle around Weeda who is now holding Rabbit's body in her arms

rocking back and forth, looking up to heaven with tears flowing down her face. The Slave Women are kissing and hugging on Weeda, Omas and Rabbit until they all fall to the ground continuing to shout and praise Jesus. They then all get up, pick Weeda, up and carry her gently to the porch. They sit Weeda down in her rocking chair and she begin to rock, smiling sadly, but as though she knows that she will grieve for a moment but because of the circumstances she must move on.

Omas leans down and kiss Weeda on her forehead. She continue to rock back and forth with a blank look on her face. Omas Kisses weeda again on the cheek.

Overseer Smith

Overseer Smith and the Slave Catchers stop and look around at the Slaves in their joy.

Good lord! Did you see that? Did you see what I just saw? First you dog them all day!

Then you kill one of them for running away, and then you dump him right in their laps, and yet, they dance and shout for joy. Instead of having sad feelings and grieving like normal civilized people would, they all just dance and shout for joy.

This is some weird race of people, if you can call them that. I'm telling you the truth, I've never seen anything like it. Well, anyway, now we can get the others out and go to work in the fields for the rest of the day.

Weeda

The Slaves standing facing the clearing, looking to a place that they know their bodies will never go.

Oh Jesus, I'm so tired. I could just sit down right here on the ground. You better run little girl!! You better run!! Run for your life!! Run for all of our lives!! Then come back some day and get some of us to run with you!!

Weeda speak under her breath with a smile creasing her tired, weather beaten face. Weeda looks at Omas and the other Slaves. Speaking to the other Slaves.

Well, I guess you all had better go on back to work. Me and Omas will take care of our boy Rabbit! We know what to do! We know.

Weeda looks at Omas and then towards heaven and smiles.

Lord we thank you!!

END OF PLAY

EULOGY

TO BE RISEN FROM PERDITION
BY
BRO. LARRY B. STEVENSON

'**RESPECT AND GREETINGS**' my brothers!   My family! Understudies of America… these United States… the nation of emigrants…land of the free, land of trickery, connivance, contempt and deceit.

'**GREETINGS AND BLESSINGS**' unto we people who seek to read, learn and understand the astonishments, the derangements, the missing literature from the literature , the old stories newly told by the tattle-tale-black writers.

'**BLESSINGS AND PRAISES**' unto we who are over due in blessings and praises; In self appraisals, self-love, self-knowledge, self- understanding, self-history.

'**PRAISES AND ENDURANCE**' unto we who have miraculously endured far surpass that which is endurable; We who have lived generations after generations, devoting entire lives, exercising our intuitions, cognitions, and wisdom by drastically choosing between the woos and woes of worse and worser…

'**ENDURANCE AND PRAYERS**' unto we who have endured and prayed chauvinistically for over two hundred years in a free land of limitations, restrictions, afflictions, and abuse.

'PRAYERS AND MINISTRY' unto who minister the eulogies of those dubbed fearful for wisely abandoning the ship/ shore ships that steals away from the shores.

'MINISTRY AND UNDERSTANDING' unto we who have lived experiences compounded upon experiences in the midst of a culture defused;

We who have learned a language of distinctions in diction, in which separate word meanings, have ofter been found to be synomous and compatible such as 'intelligence' and 'fear'.

'UNDERSTANDING AND REVIVAL' unto we whom are the renaissance-people of those non soldiers killed when/where they died the deaths of soldiers fighting for their...

'REVIVAL AND RENOVATION' unto we whom through the will to survive have achieved the essential strength,, strength to revise our minds, so that we may build, reconstruct, and grow.

'RENOVATION AND REASON' unto we who have vainly failed due to reasons in remembering to remember those who was forced to forget... remembrance of the SLAVE- SHIP- SHORE- SHIP- SHIPWRECKED.

To: brother **John H. Hall**

In tribute to **remembrance**

In tribute to **friendship**

In cordial **response to**

Your **beautiful- bitter- sad- plays**

Rev. John H. Hall
Po Box 91589
Houston, Tx. 77291

E mail address
blkmktbks@Comcast.net